Quantum Cybersecurity Program Management

Quantum Cybersecurity Program Management

Greg Skulmoski and Ashkan Memari

BEP

BUSINESS EXPERT PRESS

Leader in applied, concise business books

Quantum Cybersecurity Program Management

Cover design by Gregory Skulmoski

Interior design by Exeter Premedia Services Private Ltd., Chennai, India

First published in 2025 by
Business Expert Press, LLC
222 East 46th Street, New York, NY 10017
www.businessexpertpress.com

ISBN-13: 978-1-63742-758-3 (paperback)
ISBN-13: 978-1-63742-759-0 (e-book)

Business Expert Press Portfolio and Project Management Collection

First edition: 2025

10 9 8 7 6 5 4 3 2 1

Description

Quantum technology interest is accelerating for two key reasons: first, quantum technologies promise transformative capabilities. Indeed, quantum computing is seen as a strategic necessity by the world's leading economies. Second, experts unanimously agree that a cryptographically-relevant quantum computer will have the capability to break classical encryption that keeps our data and transactions private. Thus, organizations are challenged to protect their most sensitive information data and systems before a cryptographically-relevant quantum computer is accessible to hackers despite already over burdened cybersecurity teams.

Quantum Cybersecurity Program Management by Dr. Greg Skulmoski and Dr. Ashkan Memari is part of a series of books: *Shields Up: Cybersecurity Project Management*, which outlines a risk-based approach to cybersecurity project management including technology and process improvement projects, and *Cybersecurity Training: A Pathway to Readiness*, which outlines best practices in training and instructional design to up skill the organization's people. *Quantum Cybersecurity* builds upon *Shields Up* (technology and process) and *Cybersecurity Training* (people) to provide a program approach to deliver the diversity of quantum projects and initiatives organizations encounter.

The authors of *Quantum Cybersecurity* bring together best practices found in standards and frameworks in a risk-based approach to implementing a quantum program of projects. Tailored for quantum champions, IT security architects, business leaders, project managers, digital leadership, and board members, *Quantum Cybersecurity* offers actionable guidance. Urgent and early adopters will find a practical guide for a quick start to their quantum projects.

Contents

Testimonials

In this book, we conducted a peer review to collect feedback to find and fix any errors, identify gaps and opportunities, and clarify any ambiguous concepts. We developed a heterogeneous sample of subject matter experts from (i) project and program management, (ii) cybersecurity, and (iii) quantum technologies research, development, and implementation. We used the snowball technique to find our subject matter experts and to address any validity risks related to bias. We provided *Quantum Cybersecurity Program Management* to 15 people, and 12 of them returned constructive feedback that we incorporated. For example, we rewrote some sentences for clarity and added additional content to strengthen the main points. Thank you. Some expert reviewers also provided positive praise that we share with you.

Quantum Readiness Expertly Simplified and Decoded

"I have read many books and documents about quantum technologies having authored Quantum Nation: India's Leap into the Future, *but none have clearly laid out a practical pathway to quantum readiness. In this book, quantum readiness is expertly simplified and decoded. The figures clarify complex concepts and offer insight into reaching quantum preparedness. I really like this book."* —**L Venkata Subramaniam, PhD, IBM Quantum India Lead, IBM Master Inventor, Indian Institute of Technology, India**

No Other Resource as Comprehensive

"From my review of Quantum Cybersecurity Program Management, *I found it to be very thorough and timely with great information for organizations looking to address the VERY real challenges that quantum will undoubtedly bring to cybersecurity strategies. I know of no other resource as comprehensive. I can think of several C-level people who will love the book, as I do get asked about the "quantum threat" regularly. I keep saying—It's real, it's coming and now is the time to start understanding it."* —**Bob Dameron, Head of Business Development, Multiverse Computing, Canada**

A Wonderful Creation From the Authors of *Shields Up* and *Cybersecurity Training*

"*The* Quantum Cybersecurity *authors offer comprehensive and practical program management approach to implement complex post-quantum cryptographic migrations based on a foundation of risk, quality, project, and technology service management. A wonderful creation from the authors of* Shields Up: Cybersecurity Project Management *and* Cybersecurity Training: A Pathway to Readiness. *This book is very good and implementable reference for project managers like me when running post-quantum migration projects.*"—**Irene Corpuz, MSc, CISA, ISO 27k Lead Auditor & Lead Implementer, ITIL, PMP, PMI-ACP, Co-Founder and Board Member—Women in Cyber Security Middle East, Global Advisory Board Member—EC Council, United Arab Emirates**

Gives Actionable Steps for Project Managers, IT Managers, and Executives

"Quantum Cybersecurity Program Management *gives actionable steps for project managers, IT managers, and executives alike. Aligning with multiple standards and best practices, it ensures that readers can easily incorporate lessons learned into their current work practices and business strategies. It is a great read and I highly recommend it to all technology leaders and project managers.*"—**Jake McGaffin MBA, MEM, CSM, Project Manager, Gensco Inc., USA**

An Indispensable Guide to Quantum Readiness

"Quantum Cybersecurity Program Management *is a seminal work that masterfully addresses the imminent challenges posed by quantum technologies to modern cybersecurity frameworks. The authors, Dr. Gregory J. Skulmoski and Dr. Ashkan Memari, deliver not just a book, but a comprehensive roadmap that is both enlightening and immensely practical. Their detailed approach to integrating quantum computing into existing cybersecurity strategies is unmatched in clarity and depth.*

As someone who frequently discusses the quantum threat with industry leaders, I can affirm that this book is the definitive resource we've been waiting for. It's a compelling read for anyone who recognizes that the quantum era is on our doorstep and understands the critical need for preparedness. This is essential reading for C-level executives, IT professionals, cybersecurity experts, and especially project managers, who will find invaluable guidance for navigating the complexities of quantum project management. This book is the guide that those at the forefront of business and technology need by their side."—**Julio Bandeira de Melo, Cybersecurity Leader, Canada**

Complex Topics Masterfully Simplified and Demystified

"The authors of Quantum Cybersecurity *touch on many important topics including solid guidelines to plan, implement, and optimize quantum technologies. The book is very timely and provides practical advice for all organizations who should already be gearing up for the positive and negative impacts quantum technologies will bring. This book will help the reader catch up if they have not yet started on their quantum journey.*

Taking a project and program management approach is necessary to successfully implement quantum technologies. For the first time, trusted and proven approaches (e.g., program management) are tailored for implementing emerging technologies (e.g., post-quantum cryptographic migrations) in one book. I also like the way the authors explained the different quantum technologies and contrast them to classical computing, complex topics masterfully simplified and demystified.

Many thanks for the opportunity to read a draft copy of your book. Overall, I would purchase the book. I hope the book becomes a bestseller." —**Thomas Matheus PhD, CTO, Cystel, the United Kingdom**

A Big Win for Professionals in Cybersecurity

*"*Quantum Cybersecurity Program Management *by Gregory J. Skulmoski, PhD, and Ashkan Memari, PhD, dives into the complex world where quantum computing meets cybersecurity. It's structured to walk you through the basics and build up to the more intricate ways these fields intersect, especially through the lens of project management.*

The book doesn't shy away from the tough stuff—it's packed with technical details and theories. What stands out is how the book maps out the integration of quantum computing into cybersecurity practices, aligning with professional standards like ITIL and NIST. This practical approach is a big win for professionals in cybersecurity.

Overall, this detailed guide is perfect for professionals who want to dive deep into managing the transition to quantum-resistant cybersecurity frameworks and to stay ahead in these rapidly evolving fields."
—**Dr. James Paul, PhD, MBA, BSc CompSci, FGIA, Â MACS CP, IP3, CISM, GRCP, GRCA, CEH, ISO 270001, TOGAF 9 L2, PRINCE2 Agile, ITIL, Australia**

A Valuable Guide Grounded in Best Practices

"Quantum Cybersecurity Program Management *is a valuable guide for people preparing their organizations for the impacts and opportunities of extraordinary quantum compute power. It is well organized, full of learning resources and grounded in program and project management best practices."*—**Hilary Milana, IT Portfolio and Program Management Practice Leader, USA**

A Fine Approach I Can Use

"The book sets a strong foundation by explaining the importance of quantum technologies and their dual potentialities, highlighting the imminent risks and opportunities of quantum computing. The content strikes a balance between technical depth and accessibility, catering to both technical experts and business leaders. The book provides comprehensive strategies for business, technology, and cybersecurity transitions, emphasizing a proactive approach. The detailed sections on program and project management offer valuable insights into planning, executing, and optimizing quantum projects. The inclusion of project management best practices is particularly useful. The microlearning sections and references to further resources are excellent for readers who wish to delve deeper into specific topics. All in all, a fine approach I can use in my quantum projects."—**Simone Vernacchia, Senior Partner and Head of Technology, Telecommunications, Media, Tourism, Middle East, Deloitte**

Foreword

It's evident that new quantum breakthroughs will further transform how people work and live in the years ahead, revolutionizing industries and driving innovation.

—Hisham El-Bihbety, CISO, Bank of Canada
(Canadian Forum for Digital Infrastructure Resilience 2023, v).

Quantum Cybersecurity Program Management is written for those who are excited about quantum technologies and their promises. Who can ignore the "rapidly growing" quantum economy characterized by "hefty public and private investments" across most G20 countries (World Economic Forum 2022a, 8). However, quantum technologies can be used to break most encryption methods that currently secure sensitive data and systems. To counter these risks, *we* (the authors of this book) aim to provide guidance to migrate to post-quantum cryptography and develop cybersecurity readiness* and to reduce the learning curve with a comprehensive approach to quantum cybersecurity programs and project management.

As you read about post-quantum cryptography, you will discover the collective advice to "start preparing for the quantum threat now" (TNO†, 2023, 3) including government agencies: "A successful post-quantum cryptographic migration will take time to plan and conduct. CISA, NSA, and NIST‡ urge organizations to begin preparing now by creating quantum-readiness roadmaps, conducting inventories, analyzing risks, and

---

* We do not address cryptocurrency which is a form of digital currency and a term some may confuse with cryptography.

† TNO is the abbreviation for "Nederlandse Organisatie voor toegepast-natuurwetenschappelijk onderzoek" translated to "Netherlands Organization for Applied Scientific Research."

‡ Cybersecurity and Infrastructure Security Agency (CISA), National Security Agency (NSA), and National Institute of Standards and Technology (NIST) are all American government agencies.

engaging vendors" (NIST 2023a, 1). Specifically, organizations can transition to a secure quantum ecosystem through a series of projects and initiatives based on risk management best practices:

1. **Quantum awareness:** Build knowledge and skills in quantum technologies to deliver innovation, as well as quantum cybersecurity.
2. **Risk identification and analysis:** Conduct and maintain an inventory of the organization's use of cryptography then identify and analyze the severity of quantum risks.
3. **Risk treatment:** Identify, prioritize, budget, and implement a program of projects and initiatives to migrate to post-quantum cryptography[§] including hybrid solutions, and develop cryptographic agility (e.g., the ability to quickly update the organization's cryptography). Work with customers, suppliers, business partners, and others to develop a comprehensive approach to supply chain quantum cybersecurity and value chain optimization, including quantum awareness, risk identification, and risk treatment.[¶]

Therefore, we proceed with a risk-based approach to transition to a quantum ecosystem and to migrate to and incorporate new post-quantum cryptographic protocols, followed by continual improvement initiatives and projects.

Quantum Cybersecurity Program Management is structured into five parts. In Chapter 1, we review the burgeoning demand for quantum technologies including quantum cybersecurity. We examine quantum technologies and cryptography to better understand the technologies that will be planned, implemented, and optimized. Chapter 2 has an overview of the best practices supporting the program of quantum projects facing the organization including the Information Technology Infrastructure

---

§ When we write about post-quantum cryptographic migrations, those post-quantum cryptographic solutions are more likely to be hybrid solutions with other cryptography rather than a pure post-quantum cryptographic solution.

¶ Risk treatment is ISO 31000 Risk Management terminology, while risk response is PMBOK® Guide terminology; however, the tools and processes are mostly the same.

Library Framework (ITIL). The ITIL Framework guides organizations to plan, deliver, and optimize digital products (e.g., new robots, laptops, printers, servers) and services (e.g., e-mail, human resource information systems, pharmacy systems, cloud storage) throughout the technology lifecycle. Michele Mosca, the famed quantum risk management guru, wrote "Most importantly, a safe transition can only be achieved through technology lifecycle management—not crisis management—and will require significant time" (Mosca and Piani 2023, 4).

Chapter 2 continues with the National Institute of Standards and Technology (NIST) Cybersecurity Framework that guides organizations to provide cybersecurity. The NIST Cybersecurity Framework is widely adopted in over one hundred countries and translated into 10 languages including English, Arabic, Japanese, Spanish, Portuguese, and Polish with more promised. Therefore, *Quantum Cybersecurity* is aligned with the generally accepted NIST Cybersecurity Framework; however, those organizations following ISO/IEC 27000 Information Security series of standards, the Australian Information Security Manual, and others will also benefit from a structured transition approach to quantum readiness detailed in this book. We review the hybrid project management approach to deliver technologies, products, and services like cybersecurity. We align the ITIL Framework, NIST Cybersecurity Framework,** and project management to improve the probability of a successful transition to quantum readiness (including post-quantum cryptography and cryptographic agility).

In Chapter 3, we review best practices in strategy management and guide the reader to develop quantum strategies for business, IT, and cybersecurity functions. These aligned strategies guide the quantum technologies program, including post-quantum cryptographic migrations. In Chapter 4, the program of quantum projects is detailed including (i) minimum viable cybersecurity foundation, (ii) quantum awareness, (iii) project management optimization, (iv) service management optimization, (v) quantum technologies and applications, (vi) cryptographic agility, and (vii) post-quantum cryptographic migration projects.

** The reader may download and review the NIST Cybersecurity Framework and other documents like the Australian Information Security Manual as they are introduced and review the content.

In Chapter 5, we apply hybrid project management to deliver projects and proceed through initiation, plan, design, build, test, transition to the production environment, go-live, and project closure.

This book is written for a broad audience including:

Technology leaders: The IT security and infrastructure architects[††] and other technology leaders will appreciate the actionable migration project plan aligned with leading cybersecurity and service management standards and frameworks.

Business leaders: The business leader responsible for the organization's products and/or services will better understand how to partner with the technology teams to develop, implement, and optimize quantum use cases to achieve corporate strategies. And board members will gain an appreciation for the complexities of quantum projects and the necessity of post-quantum cryptography and quantum agility.

Project managers: The project manager will appreciate the complexities and risks of a quantum transition program involving cybersecurity, business use cases, and a quantum infrastructure resulting in more realistic and achievable plans.

Quantum champions: will get an immediate start on their quantum projects following and tailoring the approach detailed in this book. Thus, we have a diverse audience for *Quantum Cybersecurity*, where we present a program management approach to implementing quantum technologies, post-quantum cryptography, and cryptographic agility capabilities.

Finally, we include a glossary of terms, references, author biographies, and an index. There are microlearning opportunities with referrals to

---

[††] The organization might not have a security architect position but likely to have that role which may be shared among multiple people. Our use of the *security architect* term includes the technical leadership responsible for cybersecurity. We take a similar approach and use the term *IT architect* for the role of senior technical or infrastructure leadership who guides technical strategies. When in doubt, we are inclusive of inviting stakeholders to engage in our projects.

online resources for further learning about concepts presented in *Quantum Cybersecurity* (e.g., some content is dense, and some readers will find more information online to address any knowledge gaps). We take a unique approach to learning where the reader will benefit from both end-to-end readings and a focused approach to selectively review concepts to use in live projects, including near-term quantum technologies projects. The reader is rewarded with slow and contemplative reading followed by thinking about applying key concepts. Thus, this book is a reusable learning resource to improve the probability of a successful transition to quantum readiness that was developed based on best practices advocated by leading experts and organizations, as well as our own project experiences implementing emergent and beta-version technologies.

What Is Microlearning?

Traditional learning involves attending a training course for a day or two. After a few months, learning retention decays unless it is refreshed or used. With microlearning, the learner acquires additional knowledge to apply to real work. Microlearning can be more effective when the learner follows a learning to-do list and is supplemented by subscribing to online topics of interest. Learning is continual with regular influxes of small portions of content.

Microlearning

We invite you to search[‡‡] online and use other technologies to find additional information about topics of interest:

- Review best practices for generating or finding information online; the *systematic literature review* and *meta-analyses* are techniques popular with researchers to complete thorough searches,

---

[‡‡] We use the term *search online* broadly to mean using online resources and generative artificial intelligence to learn more about topics of interest. For example, the reader may *search* for project migration templates.

- Track your industry and discipline's quantum technologies transformation trends, including use case implications and emerging opportunities,
- Become familiar with privacy and cybersecurity-related regulations in your industry including any international, national, state, and city,
- Set up alerts to receive content covered in *Quantum Cybersecurity*.

Acknowledgments

When you write a book, you realize how many people have helped you to get the book into publication. The list of people to thank is long and I am fortunate to have many people guide me throughout my career and education. Mr. Le Dressay first taught me about quality during high school. Professors added more red ink to assessments than my black type, which helped me reflect, learn, and improve. My co-author Dr. Ashkan Memari is inspirational as he has a different background, rich experiences, and keen insight. The many peer reviewers who gave up evenings and weekends to diligently comment and provide constructive feedback.

The Business Expert Press team was extremely helpful and supportive including Dr. Kam Jugdev, Charlene Kronstedt, Cassie Norcutt, and Scott Isenberg. The Exeter editorial team is world-class. The talented Ben Griggs took our photos. The team members and leaders in past projects at Regina Qu'Appelle Health Region (project finance), Stream Data Systems (Y2K preparation projects), and Cleveland Clinic Abu Dhabi (complex and emerging medical technologies) showed me how to apply project management theories in a lean and practical manner. Finally, my family and friends who have been with me all along my dual career paths: project manager and academic. Thank you kindly.

Greg Skulmoski

◈ ◈ ◈

Writing a book can be both challenging and rewarding. This journey has been particularly fascinating and a unique learning experience for me, largely due to the opportunity to collaborate with Associate Professor Greg Skulmoski. Greg is not only an inspirational mentor but also a critical, kind, and detail-oriented person—qualities that are rarely found together in one individual. For this, I am deeply grateful for the opportunity of co-authorship and for his mentorship in writing this book.

I would also like to extend my heartfelt thanks to The Business Expert Press team, who was extremely helpful and supportive throughout this process. Special thanks to Dr. Kam Jugdev, Charlene Kronstedt, Cassie Norcutt, and Scott Isenberg for their invaluable assistance.

Finally, I want to express my deepest gratitude to my beautiful wife, who has always been my best friend and greatest supporter. Thank you for your unwavering love and encouragement.

Ashkan Memari

CHAPTER 1

Quantum Ecosystem

> *Quantum computers are able to perform complex calculations at 100 million times the speed of current computers* (PWC 2019, 9).

It is sometimes difficult to believe that even more innovative technologies are on the horizon, while we are implementing and adopting transformative artificial intelligence and automation technologies today. Our opening quote from PricewaterhouseCoopers International Limited (PWC) was chosen to set a historical benchmark where in 5 or 10 years, we may be measuring calculations that are trillions of times faster! Quantum technologies promise to revolutionize medicine and scientific discovery and help a struggling planet. Quantum technologies also have the potential to do great harm when threat actors harness their power. We (the authors of *Quantum Cybersecurity*) outline a program approach to plan, implement, and optimize quantum technologies and cybersecurity.

Introduction

Interest and hype have increased in quantum technologies due to the promises of unimaginable innovations as well as severe risks[*] like Encryptogeddon where the benefits of quantum technologies may be outweighed by their risks (Tett 2022). In *Quantum Cybersecurity*, we guide organizations to be proactive in their journey to leverage the benefits of quantum technologies and to strengthen their cryptographic capabilities to protect their systems and data from a crippling quantum cyberattack.

---

[*] Severe risks are determined by a qualitative risk analysis: Probability of Occurrence (High) × Impact (High) = Severe Risk.

These organizations are unique as will be their transition to a secure environment with quantum technologies. However, the risk-based approach in this book applies to most quantum technology and cryptography projects, most of the time. With tailoring and combining, the reader can quickly start their program of quantum projects, which are likely to be a "complex and delicate process" (Mosca and Piani 2023, 8).

Quantum: An Emerging Technological Revolution

Whether it is in government reports like the Australian *National Quantum Strategy 2023* or the World Economic Forum (2022a) *State of Quantum Computing: Building a Quantum Economy,* all advise quantum technologies are emerging and will be transformational; all organizations (nonprofit, private, and public) need to begin their quantum journey. We leave it to the reader to find out about the quantum economy, the key players, macroeconomic and government policy debates, quantum mechanics, quantum technologies (e.g., quantum sensing and communications), emerging regulations, and other related topics, while we focus on quantum cybersecurity and program management. But first, we address the dual potentialities of quantum technologies.

Dual Potentialities of Quantum Technologies

Technology can be used for positive and constructive or negative and harmful purposes; for example, one may use AI to create a cybersecurity training course (*constructive*) or to create a threatening email (*harmful*). The technology is neutral; it is the user that determines whether to use the technology in a *good* way (e.g., develop personalized medicine through simulations with quantum technologies) or in a *bad* way (e.g., decrypt sensitive data and gain unauthorized access with quantum technologies). Dual potentialities of technology are different from *dual-use* technologies where there may be a civilian use case (e.g., use a spreadsheet to track one's health and fitness) and a military use case (e.g., use a spreadsheet to track the enemy's movement patterns) with the same technology.

We offer a program management approach to implement *constructive* quantum technologies, as well as post-quantum-resistant cryptography to thwart hackers (*harmful*).

> *The threat posed by quantum computers could lead to a catastrophic failure of cyber-systems both through direct attacks and by disrupting trust* (Mosca and Piani 2022, 8).

The *catastrophic failure* scenario outlined by Mosca and Piani (2022) is based on a powerful enough quantum computer—a cryptographically-relevant quantum computer—using Shor's algorithm to break[†] classical Rivest–Shamir–Adleman (RSA) encryption to gain unauthorized access to sensitive data. Indeed, in the *Financial Times*, Gillian Tett (2022) warned readers that *Encryptogeddon* may occur where the negative impacts of quantum technologies outweigh the benefits of quantum technologies.

Therefore, early adopters are not only exploring quantum technologies but also transitioning to quantum-resistant algorithms—a massive program of complex projects: "Governments and businesses must act now, as quantum security risks and business opportunities cannot be ignored" (World Economic Forum 2022a, 4). Encryption is broadly used and will have to be analyzed for quantum risks: digital signatures, identity authentication process, symmetric key transport, privilege authorization processes, and so forth.

Thus, organizations will implement projects that are representative of the dual potentialities of technology: projects that will contribute to the organization's vision, goals, and objectives. The organization will also implement projects to secure systems and data including establishing a minimum viable security foundation, implementing post-quantum cryptography, and establishing cryptographic agility.

[†] We use the colloquial term *break* to mean when a cryptographic function no longer provides sufficient protection due to newly discovered design flaws or new methods of attack (e.g., apply Shor's algorithm to solve factorization problems used by classical encryption standards like RSA and AES algorithms).

Transition to a Quantum Ecosystem

The goal is to adopt and leverage quantum technologies and to safeguard data and systems from quantum risks before a cryptographically-relevant quantum computer emerges. Organizations can benefit from planning their transition to a quantum ecosystem[‡] while time is on their side. Later, we introduce a quantum risk analysis technique (using Mosca's Theorem) to determine how much time an organization may have to safely migrate and protect their data before quantum-relevant computers are available. Organizations are transitioning to quantum technologies to leverage their capabilities and disrupt their market. While quantum technologies may unlock major breakthroughs in drug discovery, gene expression-based cancer, and population care, they might be paired with artificial intelligence in tomorrow's healthcare setting:

1. **Pharmacy:** Apply combinatorial optimization[§] to improve prescription fulfillment workflows through the pharmacy to maximize scarce resources and throughput and minimize waste and waiting time.
2. **Pathology laboratory:** Maximize workflows in a hospital pathology laboratory where low-priority tests give way to high-priority tests, and again scarce resources are optimized (including laboratory specialists, equipment, and supplies), and waiting times and waste are minimized.
3. **Patient scheduling:** Optimize to maximize patient appointment opportunities and hospital bed availability, while minimizing time, resources (e.g., expertise and specialized medical equipment), and waste.

[‡] There is no general agreement for what a quantum ecosystem might look like; however, our view is it will feature quantum-relevant technologies mixed with classical computing components rather than a quantum ecosystem comprised of 100 percent quantum technologies. The quantum ecosystem will continuously evolve as is the nature of technology.

[§] Combinatorial optimization is a field of mathematics using algorithms to solve problems based on a finite set of options among competing demands or objectives to optimize schedules, resource allocation, and more.

4. **Finance:** Create a bill to optimize the amount the patient's health insurers contribute and minimize the patient's out-of-pocket expenses for healthcare services.

5. **Supply chain:** Improve demand forecasting to maximize inventory availability and minimize inventory holding costs (e.g., maximize inventory turnover Key Performance Indicators, KPIs).

6. **Caregiver training:** Optimize caregiver training scheduling so capable caregivers (e.g., valid certification in intubation procedures) are available to meet patient scheduling needs and minimize patient appointment cancelations due to resource shortages.

Early adopters in most industries and disciplines are exploring quantum technology use cases and collaborating with their IT (Information Technology) departments to implement these technologies. At the same time, IT leadership is planning risk treatment for quantum-enabled cyberattacks. Given the pervasiveness of digital technologies and their underlying public encryption, the transition to secure quantum technologies is a complex program of projects for most organizations spanning many years, perhaps decades as past cryptographic migrations were challenging, and expensive, with less pervasive technologies.

Quantum Technologies

While our focus is on project management, we briefly describe the quantum technologies organizations have begun to implement through a program of projects and initiatives.

Classical Computing

We refer to classical computing as technology that uses binary bits in the state of either a one or a zero. It is the most common type of computing used in the first quarter of the 21st century. Classical computing includes *information systems* used in accounting, human resource management, email services, customer relationship management, and other *business-oriented* systems to manage and control data. *Information technology systems* provide the infrastructure for information systems as well as for industrial control systems.

Industrial control systems also known as *operational technology* deserve special mention; these systems interact with the physical environment to monitor and control devices, processes, and events. Industrial control systems include building automation, transportation, access control, and environment monitoring (NIST 2023b, 8). Critical industries (e.g., defense, energy, healthcare, financial services, food and grocery) use industrial control systems to support critical national functions like transporting cargo and passengers by air and providing metals and materials. Therefore, industrial control systems control physical functions, while IT systems are used to manage and control data.

Classical computing is expected to continue as it can support quantum computing processing. Quantum computing is unlikely to be used for common tasks like sending emails and browsing the internet (World Economic Forum 2022a, 18). Thus, quantum and classical computers, whether industrial control or information technology systems, may work in tandem or sequentially, or they can work independently of each other resulting in greater project complexity.

Industrial control systems use software like Supervisory Control and Data Acquisition (SCADA) systems to keep our lights on and our drinking water safe. These industrial control systems provide many benefits like process automation, but they can also be attacked by cyber threat actors using classical computer technologies today and quantum technologies tomorrow posing a catastrophic risk: "With infrastructure breakdowns being one of the main concerns for cyber leaders, this places it among the highest challenges business organizations face in the future" (World Economic Forum 2022b, 10). Therefore, industrial control systems also face quantum cybersecurity risks and issues and will need to transition to post-quantum cryptography (CISA 2023a).

Indeed, the Biden administration in 2022 directed government agencies (including critical infrastructure organizations) and suppliers, to begin their journey to post-quantum cryptography and cryptographic agility "with the goal of mitigating as much of the quantum risk as is feasible by 2035" (The White House 2022, 4). Note the long lead-time (13 years) the White House has given for this complex and critical program of projects! Our project-oriented approach to transition to quantum technologies, implement quantum use cases, achieve cryptographic agility, and implement post-quantum cryptography equally applies to information systems, industrial control systems, and information technology systems.

Like technologies before them, many classical technologies will follow a predictable lifecycle where they will be displaced by more powerful and capable technologies like quantum technologies. Since the technology lifecycle is well studied, implemented, and optimized, we align with technology lifecycle management best practices (e.g., ITIL Service Management Framework described later) that increase quality and reduce risk.

Public Encryption

The source of the Encryptogeddon risk is related to how data and communications are secured so only the intended and authorized people have access to data and communications. Encryption is fundamental to all industries and sectors (Table 1.1); given the theoretical ability of a quantum computer to break public key encryption, organizations are advised to migrate to post-quantum cryptographic resistant protocols (e.g., hybrid key encapsulation where classical and quantum-resistant keys are combined). NIST has long advised to replace

Table 1.1 Encryption data examples by industry

Industry	Common Encrypted Data
Healthcare	Electronic patient record (e.g., test results), financial data (e.g., month-end report), intellectual property (e.g., research results), and so on
Defense	Strategic, operational, and tactical communications regarding current and future operations, personally identifiable information, and so on
Banking	PIN authentication, POS terminal, and ATM transactions; customer personal information, marketing, strategy, and so on
Green energy	Transmits data between SCADA devices; configuration files, event logs, and database data; command and control signals; and so on

quantum-susceptible protocols like the RSA, Menezes–Qu–Vanstone, and Diffie–Hellman algorithms (NIST 2019, 1).

The most common forms of protection are encryption and decryption, which protect the confidentiality of data and communications from unauthorized access (e.g., eavesdropping). Simply, an encryption key is used by the sender or user of the data to *lock* the data, and a decryption key is used by the receiver or user of the data to *unlock* the data. There are two common types of cryptography available in this process: symmetric-key cryptography, where both encryption and decryption keys are the same, and asymmetric-key cryptography, where the two keys are different. Of interest here is the effect a cryptographically-relevant quantum computer has on these cryptographic schemes. Grover's algorithm shows that attacks on symmetric key cryptography are quadratically faster resulting in reduced protection. Shor's algorithm shows the capability to completely break asymmetric-key cryptography (e.g., RSA encryption) at exponential speed *if* a cryptographically-relevant quantum computer is used to factor large prime numbers that keep encryption locked.

These industries and others protect their data in use, at rest, and in transit with encryption that is thought to be susceptible to a cryptographically-relevant quantum computer and the algorithms developed by Peter Shor and Lov Kumar Grover establish that public key cryptography is at risk.

Microlearning

The history of public encryption along with best practices can be found online:

- Learn about cybersecurity critical success factors like confidentiality, availability, integrity, and nonrepudiation,
- Find out more about symmetric and asymmetric encryption and the implications of *Q-Day* when a quantum-relevant computer may arrive,
- Find out why ETSI (European Telecommunications Standards Institute), IETF (Internet Engineering Task Force), ANSSI

(*Agence ationale de la Sécurité des Systèmes d'Information*), and BSI (British Standards Institution) standards organizations recommend hybrid key encapsulation methods (e.g., hybrid cryptography).

The Algorithms of Shor and Grover

Peter Shor conducted mathematical research to solve intractable (*impossible*) mathematical problems for classical computers that demonstrated the superiority of quantum computers. Specifically, Peter Shor (1994) developed an algorithm to factor large composite numbers into their prime numbers.

The implication is a cryptographically-relevant quantum computer running Shor's algorithm will be able to break asymmetric cryptographic methods by forging RSA and ECC (elliptic curve cryptography) signatures to access sensitive data and systems:

> Many of the cryptographic products, protocols, and services used today that rely on public key algorithms (e.g., Rivest-Shamir-Adleman [RSA], Elliptic Curve Diffie-Hellman [ECDH], and Elliptic Curve Digital Signature Algorithm [ECDSA]) will need to be updated, replaced, or significantly altered to employ quantum-resistant algorithms, to protect against this future threat (NIST 2023b, 1).

Joseph and his research team (2022, 238) estimate the number of noisy qubits required to break RSA 2048 cryptography is around 20 million. Cybersecurity leadership monitors qubit milestones and others as part of their risk assessment and heed the advice of the World Economic Forum (2022b, 30): "Take prudent action now to start your transition to a quantum-safe future." Indeed, the recent Regev algorithm has optimized Shor's algorithm resulting in fewer demands on quantum processing; that is, a less powerful quantum computer may be able to break classical cryptography.

In 1996, Lov Kumar Grover developed an algorithm that improves searching through unstructured data (e.g., multimedia, videos, text, audio, websites) resulting in speedier searches. The quadratic speedup (rather than linear performance in classical computing) is due to quantum physics (e.g., quantum parallelism). The result is significant speedups in database search, retrieval, data analysis, and search optimization. Unfortunately, hackers can use Grover's algorithm to break symmetric and hash cryptographic functions. Therefore, organizations can implement post-quantum cryptography to protect against quantum cybersecurity attacks using Grover's and Shor's algorithms and a cryptographically-relevant quantum computer. Thus, a cybersecurity *arms race* is occurring between organizations and individuals implementing post-quantum cryptography and hackers working to acquire and use quantum technologies.

Quantum Technologies 101

Quantum technologies (the behavior of matter and energy) can be described in terms of quantum mechanics, a mathematical representation of subatomic particles. While classical computing is based on bits, quantum technologies are based on qubits, the smallest unit of data. A fundamental difference between bits and qubits is classical computers process data sequentially, while a quantum computer can process data concurrently. That is, a bit can be either a one or a zero; however, a qubit can be both 65 percent zero and 35 percent one. The result is quantum computers are faster because quantum mathematics is different from the classical computing binary approach, and first proposed by Richard Feynman (1982) for which he won the Nobel prize for physics and led the way for future quantum researchers like Peter Shor, Lov Grover, Michele Mosca, Dario Gil, and others. Increasing the bit size in classical supercomputers increases its power linearly while increasing qubits increases computing power exponentially.

Therefore, quantum technologies are generally appealing due to the hyperspeed of computations. The benefits (and threats) of quantum technologies, including speed can be explained by quantum parallelism, superposition, and entanglement, and we leave it to the reader to explore these concepts that Albert Einstein[⁋] referred to entanglement as *spooky action at a distance.*

Building quantum computers is complex because the quantum phenomena are fragile; the surrounding environment reduces the quantum effect in a process known as decoherence. Fault-tolerant technologies are emerging to reduce the effects of decoherence—inaccurate and unreliable computations. The effective interplay between decoherence and fault tolerance is a determining factor to scale up enough qubits so a quantum-relevant computer can outperform a classical computer (e.g., quantum superiority). IT and security architects are proactively monitoring technological bottlenecks to assess the quantum threat and the urgency to implement post-quantum cryptography (later described in Mosca's Theorem).

Quantum Algorithms

A significant difference between quantum and classical computers is their algorithms (a set of calculations and rules). Quantum computers use quantum algorithms to solve problems (e.g., searching, optimizing, and simulating). Quantum algorithms use the mathematics of quantum mechanics to represent quantum elements. Quantum mathematics is different than the math used in classical computing. For example, it is like comparing a car to a helicopter; both take you from point A to point B, but a helicopter accomplishes the task in a *different* way through flight; quantum algorithms offer additional capabilities over classical computing algorithms because the math they use differs (e.g., quantum mechanics in quantum algorithms). The most famous are Shor's and Grover's quantum algorithms. Organizations face migrating to quantum-resistant algorithms before a cryptographically-relevant quantum computer arrives and we provide a hybrid project management approach in *Quantum Cybersecurity Program Management.*

[⁋]Albert Einstein wrote to Max Born in 1947 about quantum mechanics and translation from German is "physics should represent a reality in time and space, free from spooky action at a distance" [spukhafte fernwirkung]. In *The Born-Einstein letters: correspondence between Albert Einstein and Max and Hedwig Born* from 1916–1955, with commentaries by Max Born. Macmillan. 1971. p. 158.

Quantum Computers

The quantum software organizations desire are powered by quantum computers. There are multiple types of quantum computers (Palo Alto Networks Inc. 2023, 7). First, quantum annealers are available today and are the least powerful quantum computers. They face decoherence, noise, and calibration issues resulting in low adoption. The second category of quantum computing is analog quantum simulators, which are specialized computers that simulate the behavior of quantum systems, molecules, and materials in the fields of chemistry, physics, and materials science. However, they are at risk of noise and errors. Quantum computers form the third and most promising category of computers. These are challenging to build and require many qubits to become a general-purpose and reliable quantum computer.

Benefits of Quantum Computing

Organizations are enticed by the benefits and capabilities of quantum technologies, and many are re-visioning their strategies to adopt these transformative technologies. Expect to see business cases appear in the annual budget cycle of capital expenditures and operational expenditures (e.g., CapEx) to adopt quantum technologies and applications with the following rationale:

Increased speed: Some calculations can be performed faster due to quantum parallelism (where quantum qubits can exist in multiple states simultaneously). Shor's and Grover's algorithms leverage quantum parallelism to perform exponentially faster (e.g., factoring calculations). For example, an early quantum computer with the *Sycamore* quantum processor developed by Google was "156 million times faster than the world's fastest supercomputer" (France 2023, 1). The Google quantum computer can accomplish in four minutes what a supercomputer would take 10,000 years to complete (McKinsey 2023). Such speeds can provide new business opportunities triggering requests for quantum technology projects.

Combinatorial optimization: An operations research field where one finds the optimal solution for a discrete set of options with the goal to either maximize (e.g., select from a series of business opportunities to generate the most value) and/or minimize (e.g., the duration of a complex project schedule or the number of project participants[**]).

Machine learning and data analysis: Using quantum technologies and specialized algorithms like Grover's algorithm can hyper-accelerate machine learning and data analysis tasks like data classification, clustering, and pattern recognition.

Secure communications: Quantum key distribution provides ultra-secure communications since quantum mechanics guides the exchange of quantum-safe encryption keys between two parties. Rather than using mathematics as the basis for encryption, quantum key distribution uses the properties of light (photons) to provide secure encryption and decryption.

Quantum sensing: Quantum sensors (e.g., atomic clocks and quantum computing) can provide unrivaled precision with far-reaching applications like being able to measure minuscule changes in the earth's crust to forecast a significant geological event like an earthquake.

These quantum technology capabilities and others can transform organizations and are elaborated in quantum business use cases. These are the emerging technologies project teams will implement, secure, and optimize.

[**] The authors of *Quantum Cybersecurity* predict that project management and project management offices (PMOs) will be transformed with quantum combinatorial optimization capabilities including project portfolio optimization, project selection, bid and proposal development, cost/time trade-off analysis, critical path analysis and project scheduling, resource allocation, leveling, and optimization, risk management (identification, analysis, treatment, monitor, and control), Monte Carlo simulations (true random number generation), quality control (testing), and other areas dear to project teams! Graduate students will find a wide array of rewarding research projects in applied combinatorial optimization.

Technical Challenges

There are technical challenges (e.g., decoherence) to adopting quantum technologies and many are related to quantum hardware—a quantum bottleneck. IT and security architects monitor these technologies as they are milestones on the pathway to a cryptographically-relevant quantum computer. By understanding technical progress, quantum observers can better manage quantum-related risks. Quantum observers monitor technology development challenges and breakthroughs including:

Noise and error correction: Quantum computers are delicate devices susceptible to environmental interference called noise (e.g., the earth's magnetic field, local radiation, cosmic rays), resulting in computational integrity and accuracy errors. Therefore, error correction techniques mitigate[††] quantum noise, resulting in more reliable outputs over an extended period of use. Quantum fault-tolerant computers manage error correction, and the entire system is designed to perform complex calculations within an inherently noisy environment.

Scalability: It is difficult to scale up the number of qubits while achieving sufficient qubit quality (e.g., decoherence is managed) and is necessary for a cryptographically-relevant quantum computer.

Technical specialists monitor quantum technology milestones regarding advances in quantum processor speeds, as well as noise and error correction progress to predict when a cryptographically-relevant quantum computer may emerge.

With nascent technologies like quantum, there is an issue of technical ambiguity resulting in a greater project risk environment for organizations implementing quantum technologies. However, there are effective approaches to reduce risk and increase the probability of

---

[††] Mitigation refers to softening the negative harm if a risk is unable to be prevented. Therefore, prevention and mitigation in project risk management work together. Unfortunately, mitigate is sometimes incorrectly used to mean risk management or risk prevention. Our use of mitigation aligns with ISO/IEC 31001 Risk Management.

implementing a successful program of quantum projects and initia-tives—the focus of *Quantum Cybersecurity Program Management*.

Quantum Cybersecurity Risks

> *Depending upon who you believe, Y2K will either be the biggest economic disaster since 1929, or it is overblown hype intended for the sole purpose of enriching management consultants* (Hoffbuhr 1998, 6).

The World Economic Forum (2022b, 10–11) warns a cryptographically -relevant quantum computer will arrive in the near term using Shor's algorithm to break‡‡ classical RSA encryption and gain unauthorized access to sensitive data. Since encryption is broadly used, organizations need to analyze their cryptography for quantum risks: digital signa-tures, identity authentication process, symmetric key transport, privilege authorization processes, and so forth. The complexity and criticality of this cryptographic discovery project is likely to be very high for most organizations.

Quantum Cybersecurity Risk Management

There are multiple-quantum cybersecurity strategies to treat risks related to a cryptographically-relevant quantum computer used by hackers including disconnecting elements of the system from the network to isolate and secure critical data. Other recommended methods include quantum number generators, quantum key distribution, and post-quan-tum cryptography addressed in the *Risk Treatment* section of this book. Quantum experts guide us not only on how to treat risks and issues related to quantum cybersecurity but also on when to act: yesterday! We follow generally accepted risk management practices found in standards

---

‡‡ We use the colloquial term *break* to mean when a cryptographic function no longer provides sufficient protection due to newly discovered design flaws or new methods of attack (e.g., apply Shor's algorithm to solve factorization problems used by classical encryption standards like RSA and AES algo-rithms).

(e.g., ISO 31001 Risk Management) and frameworks (e.g., NIST IR 8286 Integrating Cybersecurity and Enterprise Risk Management) to treat quantum cybersecurity risks.

Start Now Imperative

> *In the best case, organizations that begin to assess their quantum-readiness now will have time to migrate their most important systems to use quantum-resistant cryptography before threat actors (and business competitors) obtain quantum computers* (Canadian Forum for Digital Infrastructure Resilience 2023, 6).

There are many reasons to begin the journey toward quantum technologies and post-quantum cryptography:

Operational necessity: Since it is widely agreed that Shor's algorithm has the potential to break previously intractable encryption, organizations that currently rely on classical encryption will need to transition to post-quantum-resistant solutions or risk the security of their systems and sensitive data.

Project criticality: Even though the risk of a cryptographically-relevant quantum computer breaking an organization's current encryption may be in the future, there is a risk today that an organization's most sensitive data (e.g., *crown jewels*, customer data) could be stolen and decrypted later. Therefore, it is critical to protect current systems and data today with a minimum viable cybersecurity foundation.

Program complexity: Experts unanimously agree that broadly implementing post-quantum cryptography "can be extremely disruptive and often takes decades to complete" (NIST 2021, 2). And migrating an organization's cryptographic systems to PQC (post-quantum cryptography) will require significant effort. Organizations should begin planning now that the effort and time needed (e.g., to investigate, analyze, plan, procure, migrate, and validate new PQC) will not be small, and it will be different for every organization[§§] (Canadian Forum for Digital Infrastructure Resilience 2023, 4). Program and project management are precisely designed to manage project criticality and complexity, reduce risk, and deliver the intended quality.

Quantum opportunities: Quantum technologies offer many capabilities like simulation and optimization that are attractive to innovators. These promising capabilities lure organizations toward quantum technologies.

Therefore, for a variety of reasons, organizations are encouraged to begin their quantum journey with a formal approach to implementing a program of projects and initiatives.

Microlearning

There is a growing body of quantum of quantum-related information online to explore and build a foundational knowledge of quantum technologies:

- Learn about current and future quantum risks,
- Find out about best practices and risk treatment/response related to projects with a high degree of criticality and complexity,
- Identify and track quantum computing milestones: (i) quantum advantage, (ii) cryptographically-relevant quantum computer, (iii) fault-tolerant technologies, and so on.

Hybrid Quantum Computing

It is likely that organizations adopting quantum technologies will go through a hybrid phase of mixed technologies (including combined classical and post-quantum cryptography) on their way to a quantum-dominant ecosystem (Figure 1.1).

[§§] *Quantum Cybersecurity Program Management* was written precisely to address these challenges with a risk-based approach organizations can apply and tailor to their program of quantum projects and initiatives.

Classical
High Performance Computing

Hybrid
Classical *and* Quantum

Quantum
Dominant

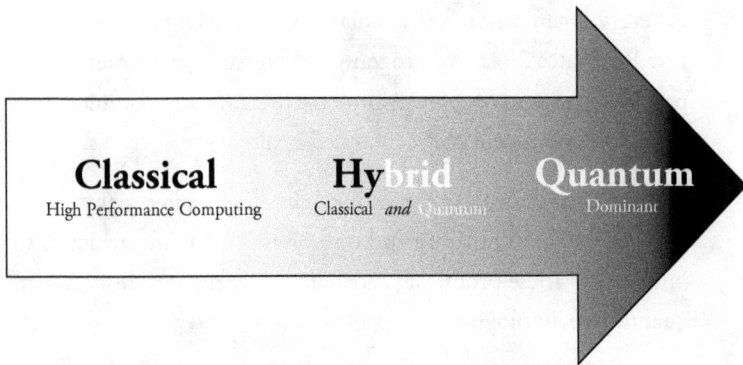

Figure 1.1 Transition to quantum technology phases

The future environment will become more *quantum-dominant* in that classical technologies are tuned to support and work in tandem with the mature quantum technical environment. The first phase of quantum transitions will likely be to a hybrid environment of classical and quantum technologies and cryptographic protocols.¶ Transitioning from a classical through to a hybrid quantum environment requires a holistic program of projects (e.g., people, process, and technology projects). Our focus is to outline a program of projects and initiatives to transition to a hybrid environment of technologies with post-quantum cryptographic solutions and cryptographic agility capabilities.

Adopting Quantum Technologies

Some organizations are early adopters of technologies like quantum technologies for their benefits and innovation opportunities. Some industries are often late adopters of technology, like power generation facilities that use long-life technologies and are infrequently upgraded compared to banking, healthcare, and defense industries. Therefore, the timing of quantum ecosystem adoption may vary by industry

---

¶ For a real example of combining classical and post-quantum cryptographic protocols, the reader is directed to Apple's PQ3 messaging protocol that combines post-quantum CRYSTALS-Kyber-1024 key encapsulation with a classical 256 Elliptic Curve key agreement. Also significant is Apple's acceptance of quantum technologies becoming mainstream (Apple Security Engineering and Architecture 2024).

and discipline. However, leadership in all industries should identify, analyze, treat, and monitor quantum-related risks sooner rather than later.

Quantum Ecosystem Drivers

The global interest in quantum computing has expanded across most industries; especially those that provide critical functions like healthcare, energy, and defense. There are many drivers to adopt quantum technologies including:

Technological obsolescence: Quantum technologies are likely to displace many classical computing technologies as it is the common way of technological obsolescence: technologies eventually become outdated, less useful, and second-rate when compared with newer, more capable alternatives like quantum technologies. Some long-lived systems have technical architectures that will be impossible to *update* to post-quantum or hybrid cryptography and instead will need to *replace* systems. Therefore, organizations with long-lived systems like those in some critical infrastructure industries (e.g., wastewater treatment) will also need to manage risks and issues related to post-quantum cryptography and cryptographic agility.

Quantum cyberattacks: Quantum cyberattacks using quantum technologies can apply brute force to potentially break classical encryption methods like AES (Advanced Encryption Standard) and RSA in less than one minute[***] (Pupillo et al. 2023, 22). A related cyberattack is when data may be manipulated resulting in negative effects like breaking cryptocurrencies or inappropriately triggering a process (e.g., opening the floodgates of a water

---

[***] Here is the calculation: "Let's imagine we have a quantum computer with 4099 qubits that are completely stable and error-free, and this quantum computer can execute a modest one million operations per second. With this quantum computer, instead of it taking 317 trillion years to break RSA 2048 as on a classical computer, this could be executed in 10 seconds" (Baumhof 2019).

dam). Data integrity degradation is also a risk treated with a minimum viable cybersecurity foundation followed by post-quantum cryptography migration projects.

Steal now, decrypt later risk: Related to brute force attacks in the future, today threat actors can steal classically encrypted data, and decrypt it later when quantum-relevant technologies become available. Sensitive information can be stolen today and unlocked in the future with a powerful enough quantum computer. Should sensitive information (e.g., state secrets, medical records, military intelligence, bank details) with a long shelf life become public, the impacts can be severe. Therefore, early adopter organizations are actively treating this risk with a minimum viable cybersecurity foundation. This risk is also referred to as *store now, decrypt later* and *harvest now, decrypt later*.

Regulatory forces: Many governments are implementing legislation to assist and compel the transition to post-quantum cryptography and cryptographic agility. Therefore, if not enticed by post-quantum cryptographic migration incentives, legislation may trigger lagging organizations to adopt post-quantum cryptography.

Market forces: Some organizations may embark on a post-quantum cryptographic migration program to remain in a preferred partner's supply chain. They may align their transition plans with the dominant member of their ecosystem or potentially lose membership. Risk-aware organizations may become early adopters and collaborate with external providers to migrate to post-quantum cryptography. They avoid the risk of a shortage of competent post-quantum cryptographic migration consultants already engaged on competitor's projects.

Industry or market disrupters: Organizations may become more competitive and gain market share by implementing quantum-business cases that disrupt and dominate an industry or a market (ITIL—Information Technology Infrastructure Library —addresses digital disruption in their strategy management practice).

Given that Shor demonstrated mathematically[†††] that classical computing cryptographic algorithms may be compromised, it is an operational necessity to transition to post-quantum cryptography to keep secure the organization's sensitive data and systems. Therefore, there are at least three implications for the organization:

1. All organizations will eventually need to migrate to post-quantum cryptography.
   a. Recommendation: Add a post-quantum cryptographic transition plan to the IT and cybersecurity strategies.
2. The migration program will take many years and require substantial resources (e.g., people, time, and money) to successfully complete this highly impactful, complex, and sustained program of projects; indeed, the migration may be cumbersome and risky which *Quantum Cybersecurity Program Management* mitigates.
   a. Recommendation: Add a quantum transition plan to the cybersecurity strategy.
3. Some hardware and devices will not support post-quantum cryptography and will need to be replaced. Since post-quantum cryptography requires powerful hardware, the organization may need to implement hardware-refresh projects (e.g., new post-quantum cryptographic-compliant technologies). The World Economic Forum (2022b, 12) estimates that approximately 20 billion devices will need to be either upgraded or updated with post-quantum cryptography resulting in many more projects!

Organizations may have multiple drivers to consider and manage leading to quantum business use case development prior to funding and approval to proceed.

[†††] While there is long-standing acceptance of Shor's algorithm (published in 1996), it is not until a cryptographically-relevant quantum computer successfully applies Shor's algorithm to factor prime numbers and break classical encryption that we can conclusively state the algorithm is *proven*.

Quantum Business Use Cases

Organizations—private, public, and nonprofit—are investigating and experimenting with quantum technologies exactly like in technology lifecycle theories and previous technology adoption practices. Early adopters increasingly create a demand for quantum technologies followed by more quantum-related products and services offered to the market. The effect will be more quantum champions inviting their IT colleagues to planning meetings and later to review quantum use cases (e.g., applying quantum technologies to financial forecasting or manufacturing optimization). Quantum uses cases are part of a quantum business case to gain leadership approval and funding. Crafting business cases is a perennial MBA topic with an enormous amount of information online to guide additional learning. The reader may also explore quantum use case guides (CEN-CENELEC Focus Group on Quantum Technologies 2023; Radwin and Hussein 2020) to better understand the *demand* component of quantum technologies. We advise readers to frame their quantum business and use cases within the ITIL Framework to improve communications, reduce risks, and achieve the desired level of quality (e.g., detailed later in ITIL Service Strategy practice).

Microlearning

IT departments exist to support business objectives and customers. Therefore, implementing a quantum program of projects is linked back to the business strategy and business use cases:

- Find online quantum use cases for your industry and discipline and learn about their scope and structure,
- Contact vendors about their quantum roadmap and how it may impact future upgrade projects,
- Identify how your industry's regulatory landscape is impacted by quantum technologies.

Quantum Risks

Those developing quantum strategies (e.g., business, technology, and cybersecurity functions) do so in an environment with associated risks that can be treated to reduce the organization's enterprise risk exposure. All organizations face common quantum risks:

Timing uncertainty: Due to the uneven progress of technology, there is a risk that a cryptographically-relevant quantum computer capable of breaking classical cryptography may arrive sooner than expected, resulting in data and systems vulnerability. For example, will quantum technologies progress at an even pace, or will there be a *sudden* step-development where a new technology revolutionizes current practices as we saw with the introduction of ChatGPT generative artificial intelligence late in 2022? There is a risk that the longer an organization waits to migrate to post-quantum cryptography, the greater the probability the organization may be unprepared and perhaps defenseless to a quantum-assisted cyberattack (TNO 2023, 7).

It may already be too late: Due to the long life of some data (e.g., personally identifiable information or state secrets), there is a risk that threat actors may steal sensitive data and wait until a cryptographically-relevant quantum computer is available to them to decrypt the stolen data, resulting in the organization's most sensitive data being breached. Communications through a public internet infrastructure (e.g., data in transit) are especially susceptible to this risk. It may already be too late for organizations that keep long-life (multidecade) information like financial or personal health information. When the information's lifespan is longer than the time for a cryptographically-relevant quantum computer to arrive, then the impact may be severe for a steal now, decrypt later risk if an organization's cybersecurity is insufficient. Therefore, long-life data and keys should be protected now through a minimum viable cybersecurity foundation project (TNO 2023, 7). The earlier an organization protects sensitive data with a minimum viable cybersecurity foundation, the sooner it will be able to stop threat actors in the future from stealing and decrypting their harvested data. Adding the previous timing uncertainty risk to the risk of starting too late is an example of a compound risk that Mosca and Piani (2023, 5) termed intolerable: "The expert responses we collected suggest that the quantum threat might rise to prominence much faster than many might anticipate. ... We note that, depending on the risk tolerance and needs of companies and institutions, such estimates may correspond already to an intolerable risk that needs to be mitigated through immediate action." This book guides the reader to reduce the severity of compound risks.

Unstable post-quantum cryptography: Since first-generation technologies often require stabilizing updates, there is a risk these early quantum-resistant algorithms may require updates that address vulnerabilities, resulting in the organization having to update their cryptography through sprints or more formal projects. Therefore, organizations are encouraged to develop cryptographic agility capabilities to quickly update and harden the algorithms protecting their data (TNO 2023, 7). Achieving sufficient quantum cybersecurity readiness will require most organizations a decade of projects encompassing people upskilling, processes optimization, and technology projects to migrate to post-quantum cryptography with cryptographic agility capabilities. A very complex, yet critical program of projects is facing most organizations. Indeed, previous cryptographic migrations (Elliptic Curve Cryptography) in less connected times took over two decades to gain widespread adoption (Joseph et al. 2022, 239).

Man-in-the-middle: An attacker uses a cryptographically-relevant quantum computer to intercept or change a message in transit without the knowledge of the sender and receiver (e.g., make changes to a contract, proposal, design specification).

Late adoption risk: Since some organizations' risk propensity is to adopt technologies after innovators and early adopters, there is a risk that competitors may be early adopters of quantum technologies, resulting in the organization losing market share to competitors who are first to leverage quantum technologies.

Quantum Cybersecurity Program Management guides the reader to prevent and mitigate these and other risks by aligning to best practices found in standards and frameworks. It is inevitable that humankind will be impacted by quantum technologies. Some organizations will be early adopters, while others prefer to follow and let others resolve issues related to the initial versions of quantum technologies.

Adopting quantum technologies and migrating to post-quantum cryptography are project-intensive activities perhaps resulting in a major organizational repositioning to lead, manage and govern. The quantum journey is more predictable, less risky, and of the right quality when aligned with global best practices found in standards and frameworks.

Microlearning

The essence of cybersecurity, program, project, and service management is risk and issue management. Therefore, learning about risk management in general, and those related to quantum projects like previous cryptography migrations can improve the probability of successful program, project, and initiative management:

- Learn about the migration from Secure Hash Algorithm (SHA)-1 to SHA-256 cryptography, with an emphasis on lessons learned, and key risks and issues related to the post-quantum cryptographic migration program of projects and initiatives,
- Discover which quantum-relevant professional certifications are available ranging from risk management (nontechnical) to programing (technical) to further enhance your skill sets.

CHAPTER 2

Quantum Transition Best Practices

In *Quantum Cybersecurity*, we align with best practices to (i) guide the quantum journey including transitioning from vulnerable to resistant post-quantum cryptography, (ii) develop cryptographic agility, and (iii) implement the transformative opportunities offered by quantum technologies to organizations and society. One of the early projects we recommend is to launch a quantum awareness program to create interest and commitment.

Quantum Awareness

To transition from a classical to a quantum-relevant ecosystem will take many years but the first step is clear:

> The primary task of most readers who are in charge of decreasing cybersecurity risk is for their organization to formally recognize the challenges posed by a post-quantum world and get senior management support for a post-quantum project as a top priority (Cloud Security Alliance 2021, 15).

While we know how to start our quantum journey, it is far from easy to influence an organization to fund and implement a decade-long cybersecurity program, while cybersecurity teams are already fully engaged with near-term activities, and their budgets are stretched!

The goals will be to increase the organization's awareness of the opportunities and risks posed by quantum technologies (dual potentialities of technology), upskill to leverage those technologies, and progress toward post-quantum cryptography and cryptographic agility. Later, we provide additional details to implement cybersecurity awareness projects. The foundation of these awareness projects, and more generally, all quantum projects, is to align with the best practices found in standards and frameworks. Indeed, the value proposition in these standards (e.g., ISO 31000 Risk Management) and frameworks (e.g., National Institute of Standards and Technology [NIST] Cybersecurity Framework) is if the user (or the organization) apply, tailor, and combine their approaches, the user (or the organization) will have fewer risks and provide the right quality.

Technical Frameworks and Standards Alignment

The transition to quantum technologies and post-quantum cryptography begins with creating a solid foundation that contributes to project leanness and sustainability; this foundation is found in international standards and frameworks. It is counter-intuitive an organization can implement a secure quantum ecosystem on time and on budget with a weak foundation of service, project, and cybersecurity management. Each industry has additional technical frameworks and standards that guide organizations to provide their goods and services according to best practices. Standards like those from the International Organization for Standardization (ISO) outline best practices for quality (e.g., ISO 9001), safety requirements for industrial robots (ISO/FDIS 10218-1), point of care laboratory testing (ISO 15189:2022), and many others.

While standards are usually rigid and accepted globally as best practices, they allow for tailoring to fit the organization's needs. Frameworks (e.g., ITIL service management) also represent best practices but usually exist without well-defined and globally accepted standards. Frameworks are less prescriptive and more flexible than standards. However, robust and widely accepted frameworks (e.g., NIST Cybersecurity Framework) may coexist with standards (e.g., ISO/IEC 27000 Information Security series) as both have risk management at their core.

The value proposition (the *Golden Promise*) is if the user (or the organization) judiciously applies the standard or framework, you (or the organization) are more likely to achieve the right quality while minimizing risks. Therefore, to transition to a quantum ecosystem, we align with best practices in global standards and frameworks (Table 2.1).

Table 2.1 Quantum cybersecurity best practices (partial list)

Name	Best Practice
A Guide to the Project Management Body of Knowledge (PMBOK® Guide)	Standard
PRINCE2 (project management from AXELOS)	Method
Agile Practice Guide (PMI)	Standard
ISO 9001 Quality Management	Standard
ISO 31000 Risk Management Series	Standard
NIST Cybersecurity Framework	Framework
NIST Migration to Post-Quantum Cryptography: NIST SP 1800-38A Preliminary Draft	Framework
NIST IR 8286 Integrating Cybersecurity and Enterprise Risk Management (ERM)	Framework
NIST SP 800-131A Rev. 2 Transitioning the Use of Cryptographic Algorithms and Key Lengths	Framework
ISO/IEC 27000 Information Technology - Security Techniques Series	Standard
Information Technology Infrastructure Library (ITIL) for Service Management	Framework
Control Objectives for Information and Related Technologies (COBIT) Technology Governance Framework	Framework

While we use the PMBOK® Guide standard for project management, we could have used another framework like PRINCE2. Or we may have used ISO/IEC 27001 Information Security, Cybersecurity, and Privacy Protection rather than the NIST Cybersecurity Framework. They are similar because each is grounded in risk and quality management best practices.

And there are other standards and frameworks to choose from that are industry specific (e.g., HIPAA to protect sensitive patient health information and ISA/IEC 62443 series for industrial automation and control systems security). The frameworks and standards we use represent best practices and are generally accepted and applicable to most projects in most industries and disciplines most of the time. The NIST Cybersecurity Framework in *Quantum Cybersecurity* is freely available in multiple languages, widely adopted, and has the robust support of the American government evidenced by regular updates and special publications.

Ultimately, no single framework will comprehensively match every operational context. The best frameworks permit themselves to be tailored to the context. We urge practitioners to rely on their experience and judgment in adopting, tailoring, and combining the most relevant components to their projects and organization with a goal of applying a minimum viable foundation of standards and frameworks.

Information Technology Infrastructure Library

Organizations provide personal productivity tools like spreadsheets, through to specialized applications used in smart warehouses, intelligent transportation, manufacturing, surgical theatres, and cost management. These and other digital services are provided by IT departments. IT departments plan, implement, manage, and optimize digital services like quantum technologies by following the ITIL framework. While other digital services frameworks and standards (e.g., COBIT and ISO/IEC 20000 Information Technology Service Management) exist, ITIL might be the most popular and widely adopted.[*]

ITIL Overview

ITIL is a framework of best practices to deliver, manage, and optimize an evolving suite of digital products and services through their life cycles. ITIL provides a comprehensive, holistic, and systematic approach to deliver value and manage risks and quality. Organizations can tailor ITIL practices and combine them with other best practices to provide a predictable and stable technical ecosystem to support quantum technologies. The ITIL way of delivering and managing technology is one of the most globally popular frameworks and, therefore, can be considered the global de facto best practice (Tsunoda and Kino 2018, 1). ITIL's popularity is due to its benefits, like increased productivity and digital performance, improved predictability, value realization and customer satisfaction, reduced costs, better return on digital investments, and enhanced communication through common

---

[*] ITIL is more fully explained and combined with project management in *Shields Up: Cybersecurity Project Management*.

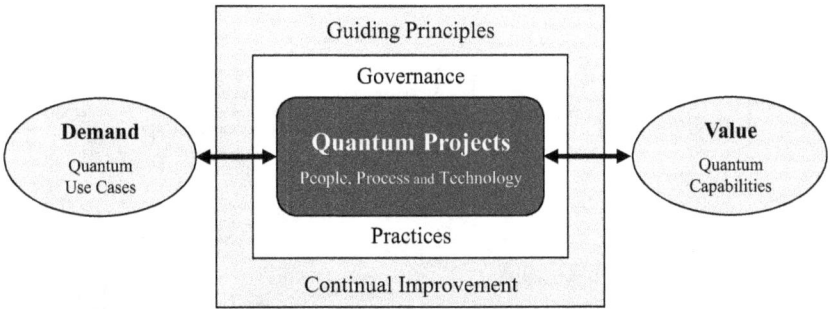

Figure 2.1 ITIL service value system for a quantum ecosystem

concepts, processes, and terminology. ITIL is a lean and widely adopted[†]
approach to technology service management. However, those practitioners following the COBIT approach to technology management can also
benefit from our approach.

Quantum Projects the ITIL Way

ITIL-aligned organizations apply the ITIL Service Value System (Figure
2.1) and tailor the framework to their unique organization. The Service
Value System outlines how to initiate, implement, deliver, and optimize digital products and services like quantum technologies (AXELOS
2019, 66). The expectation is organizations tailor the ITIL Framework
when they apply it to their unique circumstances. The Service Value
Chain process begins with a demand for a new service like quantum
technologies or to migrate to post-quantum cryptography.

A quantum project (known as the *Service Value Chain* in ITIL
terminology) is initiated, planned, designed, built/configured, tested,
and handed over to IT operations to release the service to end users
(e.g., use the quantum technology as described in the business use case).
IT operations manages the quantum technologies to enable end users to
derive value (e.g., materials simulation, a business benefit). The IT team

---

[†] Organizations vary the amount and formality of ITIL adoption. Some
implement core practices like service and strategy management, while others
implement a mature and comprehensive service management approach
outlined in the ITIL practices. Therefore, most organizations have knowingly,
or not, used some degree of ITIL service management.

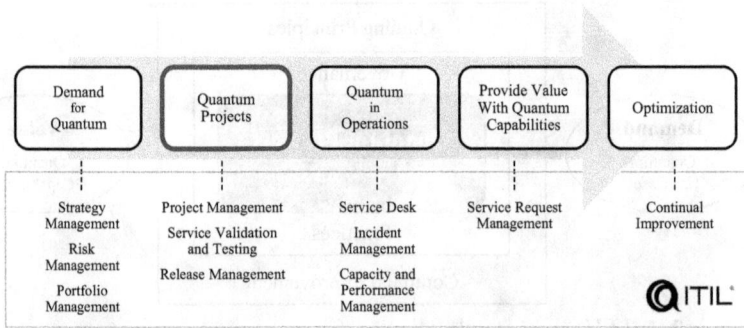

Figure 2.2 ITIL practices support quantum technology management

maintains and continually improves the digital products and services they manage.

ITIL Service Management for Quantum Technology Management

ITIL includes *practices* (e.g., strategy management, project management, continual improvement) that guide IT teams and others to provide valued digital products and services like quantum technologies (Figure 2.2). The ITIL Strategy Management practice guides the organization to tailor, combine, and implement an IT services strategy valued by their customers. Adopting and tailoring the ITIL Framework can also improve quality and reduce risks for information systems that are used to collect, store, organize, distribute, and dispose of the organization's information. Some of the other ITIL practices are also seen in Figure 2.2, such as Service Validation and Testing and Release Management, which support the project management practice.

We apply the ITIL Framework and practice processes to implement classical and quantum *information technologies* like servers and networks and *information systems* like supply chain applications. ITIL can be used to manage *industrial control systems* (a collection of technologies and instrumentation) to manage and control industrial functions and processes. Industrial control systems (also known as operational technologies) are broadly used in oil and gas transportation, water treatment, power grids, chemical plants, and more. *Quantum Cyberse-*

curity is applicable to projects in all three categories of systems: IT, information systems, and industrial control systems.

The project manager follows ITIL's practices like project management (or the more detailed PMBOK® Guide) and tests new technologies by following and tailoring ITIL's Service Validation and Testing practice. ITIL's Release Management practice guides the project and release managers to bring the new quantum product or service safely and securely to the end users. ITIL's Continual Improvement practice guides the IT department to improve its products and services like quantum technologies. ITIL practices align with the project management standard outlined in the PMBOK® Guide and ISO information security, risk, and quality management standards. The processes within these practices can be optimized for quantum projects and initiatives, and supported with templates, checklists, and training to improve the probability of success.

Finally, organizations might apply ITIL's Information Security Management (ISM) practice to secure their data and systems. This practice aims to safeguard the information the organization uses to conduct business by following the ISM process (Figure 2.3). The ITIL approach to cybersecurity begins with cybersecurity planning followed by implementing the plan. The organization evaluates the effectiveness of the cybersecurity plan, followed by optimization. The ITIL approach may be broadly applied and tailored to cybersecurity and cryptographic agility projects and post-quantum cryptographic migrations. The organization monitors their projects (Service Value Chain) and takes controlling actions if necessary (governs). Notice the ISM process (designed to keep quality high and risks low) mirrors the Deming Cycle (plan, do, check, and act) for quality management!

ITIL's ISM practice guides teams to understand and manage information confidentiality, integrity, and availability risks (CIA Triad,[‡] discussed later in Figure 2.7). The CIA Triad also appears in the ISO/IEC 27001 ISM standard and the NIST Cybersecurity

---

[‡] The CIA Triad originated to define the focus of cybersecurity; today, confidentiality, integrity, and availability are critical success factors for data security along with other cybersecurity functions like governance.

Plan	Implement
Plan Design-in Security and Risk Management	**Implement** Technical and Non-technical Quantum Cybersecurity
Maintain Maintain and Optimize Quantum Cybersecurity	**Evaluate** Security Management

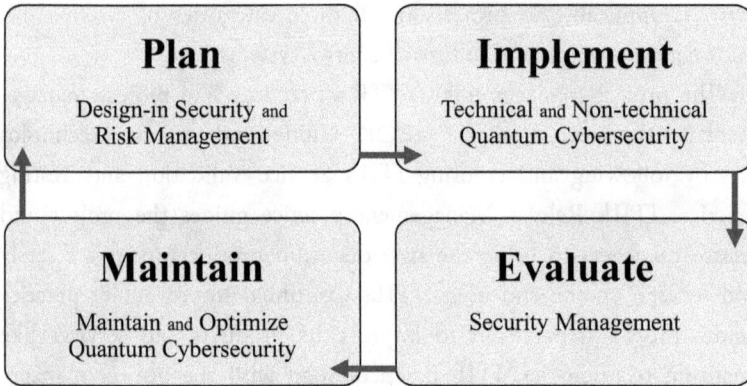

Figure 2.3 ITIL information security management process

Framework's Data Security category. At their core, these standards and frameworks are aligned and provide best practice guidance for organizations to apply, tailor and combine.

Thus, ITIL is a holistic and comprehensive framework for managing technology services such as quantum cybersecurity projects. ITIL supports tailoring the framework to the organization, context, and project; the ITIL Service Management Framework can be used with a variety of delivery approaches like hybrid project management, agile, DevOps, DevSecOps, and Lean, as well as traditional/waterfall project management (AXELOS 2019, 17). The *Golden Promise* that brings all these frameworks and standards together is if the end user correctly applies, tailors, and combines the standard or framework, the end user (or the organization) is more likely to deliver the right quality while preventing risks (discussed later, Figure 2.14).[§] Add the *Goldilocks Principle* where just the right amount of the standard or framework is applied and tailored to arrive at a lean approach, not too much, nor too little of the framework or standard (e.g., a minimum viable service management foundation to deliver the intended value).

The ITIL approach to technology management, including quantum, provides a structured and proven approach to implement, manage,

[§] The reader may substitute the ISO/IEC 27000 Information Security series of standards for the NIST Cybersecurity Framework used in *Quantum Cybersecurity*.

and optimize technologies. ITIL provides the digital foundation for organizations to provide value through technology. Therefore, organizations are encouraged to provide a minimum viable technology management foundation to adopt quantum technologies, and the ITIL Framework provides such a foundation. While ITIL has the ISM practice to address cybersecurity, the NIST Cybersecurity Framework is more detailed and comprehensive and is examined next.

NIST Cybersecurity Framework for Quantum Technologies

Most cybersecurity frameworks are based on risk and quality management; therefore, cybersecurity frameworks share common elements like principles, values, processes, tools, competencies, technologies, and governance aimed at delivering products and services at the appropriate level of quality while minimizing risks. In *Quantum Cybersecurity*, we use the NIST Cybersecurity Framework as it applies to any industry or sector of any size, whether domestic or international (NIST 2024, 2). The United States Department of Commerce makes the NIST Cybersecurity Framework freely available in multiple languages with regularly updated documents (e.g., look for updated control documents to reflect quantum technologys emergence). NIST has taken the lead and is evaluating post-quantum cryptographic algorithms and providing a transition to quantum technologies guidance.

However, whether the framework is NIST or another framework or standard (ISO/IEC 27000 Information Security series), the fundamental principles, processes, and tools outlined in *Quantum Cybersecurity* can guide organizations to adopt quantum technologies. In this book, we align with the NIST Cybersecurity Framework and are guided by its Core elements.

NIST Framework Core

The NIST Framework Core elements include six cybersecurity functions (goals) and, categories and subcategories (desired outcomes). The value

Table 2.2 NIST cybersecurity framework functions and categories

Govern	Identify	Protect	Detect	Respond	Recover
Organizational context	Asset management	Awareness and training	Continuous monitoring	Incident management	Incident recovery plan execution
Risk management strategy	Risk assessment	Identity management, authentication, and access control	Adverse event analysis	Incident analysis	Incident recovery communication
Cybersecurity supply chain risk management	Improvement	Data security	—	Incident response reporting and communication	—
Roles, responsibilities, and authorities	—	Platform security	—	Incident mitigation	—
Policy	—	Technology infrastructure resilience	—	—	—
Oversight	—	—	—	—	—

proposition is organizations can tailor their cybersecurity strategy and operations based on these six functions and systematically improve their cybersecurity capabilities. Thus, the NIST Framework Core guides organizations (Table 2.2) with cybersecurity functions (6), categories (22), and subcategories (106).

Organizations will see a continuous flow of projects and initiatives to improve these NIST cybersecurity functions as new technologies are introduced into digital ecosystems and will benefit from optimized technology lifecycle flows.

NIST Implementation Tiers

The NIST Cybersecurity Framework includes four implementation tiers that offer cybersecurity improvement and target state guidance (Figure 2.4, after NIST 2024, 7–8, 24–25). Fundamentally, one progresses through the tiers when cybersecurity risk management improves, becomes more integrated, and has active external stakeholder engagement. Organizations are more likely to move through the tiers if there is a structured and enterprise approach to cybersecurity management (people, process, and technology). The pathway to cryptographic agility and post-quantum cryptographic readiness is a planned progression through the NIST tiers and can be informed by the results of

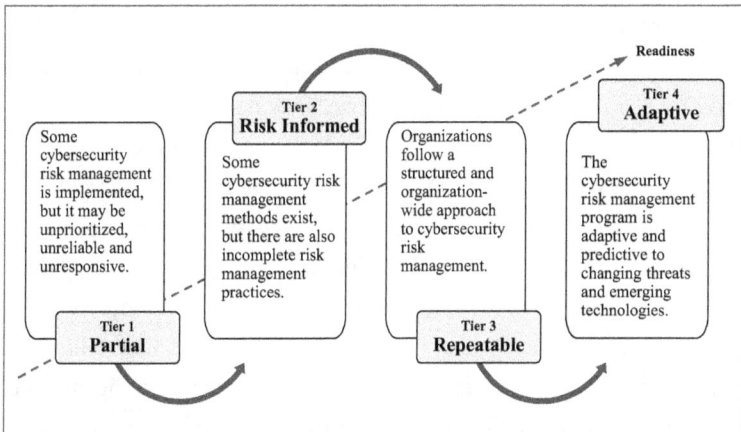

Figure 2.4 NIST implementation tiers

a cryptographic inventory discussed later. The cybersecurity maturity progression is supported when the organization's technology service management (ITIL) and project management maturity. Combined, the organization strives for a lean approach to manage technologies including quantum and cybersecurity.

Organizations can implement a program of projects and initiatives to mature and improve their cybersecurity capabilities to address any steal now, decrypt later risks, and progress toward cryptographic agility. Readers may review the Cybersecurity Capability Maturity Model (C2M2) for additional insight into maturity pathways (Office of Cybersecurity, Energy Security, and Emergency Response, 2022). NIST (2023c) has provided a map between the NIST Cybersecurity Framework and the Cybersecurity Capability Maturity Model to provide additional guidance to optimize cybersecurity.

NIST Framework Profiles

The NIST Cybersecurity Framework guides the reader to conduct a cybersecurity gap analysis as part of improving their cybersecurity posture (NIST 2024, 7). The organization can analyze its current business objectives, threat environment, and requirements/controls and use the NIST Cybersecurity Framework to arrive at its *current state* profile (Figure 2.5). The current state or profile includes the outcomes the organization is currently achieving or attempting to achieve and a measure of the degree of achievement.

The organization can identify and plan to achieve the improved *target state*. The target or future state includes the prioritized outcomes (e.g., post-quantum cryptography in a hybrid cryptographic environment with cryptographic agility capabilities). The target state also includes business, technology, and other cybersecurity objectives (adapted from NIST 2023d, 16). Indeed, an organization can have multiple profiles addressing different cybersecurity risks with different probabilities of occurrence and impact levels (e.g., the detect function may be weaker than the response function) and prioritized for improvement. The organization's cybersecurity capabilities will be reflected in

Target State

Quantum Projects

1. Cybersecurity Minimum Foundation
2. Quantum Awareness
3. Project Management Optimization
4. Service Management Optimization
5. Cryptographic Agility
6. Quantum Technologies Implementation
7. Post-Quantum Cryptographic Migrations

Improved
Cybersecurity
Readiness

Value

Gaps and
Opportunities
Identified

Demand

Current State

Figure 2.5 NIST profiles—quantum program management adaptation

the current state, and improvements through projects and initiatives will bring the organization to their target state.

In addition to quantum projects and initiatives, there may also be minimum viable foundation and no-regret cybersecurity projects and initiatives. Minimum viable foundation projects are those projects that bring an organization to a minimum state of technical maturity. The *Goldilocks Principle* implies not too much, nor too little—a minimum viable foundation. For example, Australia recommends organizations adopt the *Essential Eight* cybersecurity strategies to arrive at a *baseline* (Australian Signals Directorate 2022). Other countries have similar guides like the American CISA (Cybersecurity and Infrastructure Security Agency, 2023b) *Cybersecurity Performance Goals* to guide organizations to implement sound cybersecurity practices including a minimum foundation. It is counterintuitive that an organization can implement quantum cybersecurity without first building a solid cybersecurity foundation and implementing the basics like the *Essential Eight*. A minimum viable cybersecurity foundation is one that at least protects the organization against *steal now, decrypt later* risks.

No-regret projects are those that are cost-effective projects under a range of future risk scenarios where value is likely delivered. For example, strengthening cybersecurity incident reporting capabilities (internal and external) is likely a no-regret project for most critical infrastructure organizations because emerging regulations generally tighten cybersecurity incident reporting obligations (Department of Home Affairs 2024, 6). Therefore, some quantum projects may be no-regret projects as part of the organization's IT and cybersecurity strategies.

NIST Cybersecurity Framework Summary

The NIST Cybersecurity Framework and family of documents can guide technology teams to plan, develop, implement, and optimize their cybersecurity, including migrating to a secure quantum ecosystem. The NIST Cybersecurity Framework and supporting documents are meant to be tailored and combined to meet the organization's unique needs. Again, the *Golden Promise* applies: judiciously apply and tailor the NIST Cybersecurity Framework, and the end user (or the organization) is more likely to reduce risk and meet the desired quality levels. Thus, users are invited to tailor and implement the NIST Cybersecurity Framework according to their priorities as we do in *Quantum Cybersecurity*. The flexibility and broad applicability of the NIST Cybersecurity Framework is one of many reasons *Quantum Cybersecurity Program Management* aligns with the NIST Cybersecurity Framework and companion documents and special publications.

Other NIST Frameworks

The NIST Cybersecurity Framework is but one document organizations use to guide their projects and initiatives to provide cybersecurity readiness. NIST has released and will release updates related to the emerging quantum ecosystem such as cryptographic discovery (NIST 2023e) and testing draft standards (NIST 2023f).

NIST Cybersecurity Training

The NIST family of documents also includes cybersecurity general awareness (NIST 2003) and specialized or role-based training (NIST 2014). Cybersecurity general awareness training programs include content to shape or shift the organization's culture like the cybersecurity training one receives upon joining a new organization (e.g., *cybersecurity is everyone's responsibility* message). A learner may also receive role-based training if the person has a specialized or crucial role in cybersecurity (e.g., privileged users or executives and officers). The NIST general awareness and specialized cybersecurity training frameworks will evolve as the quantum ecosystem evolves based on NIST's commitment to supporting quantum technologies and updating their resources.

Quantum Transition

NIST has committed to support the migration to post-quantum cryptography with future *special publications* with implementation guidance, interoperability lessons, hybrid implementation solutions, and more. Therefore, we recommend the reader sign up for NIST alerts to receive notifications of new content that may be helpful to their projects. Additionally, receiving NIST updates helps understand when a cryptographically-relevant quantum computer might arrive (a critical element of Mosca's Theorem to evaluate risk addressed later).

NIST Controls

NIST regularly updates control documents that provide detailed guidance regarding the cybersecurity functions (e.g., protect, detect, recover). The NIST (2022a) Special Publication 800-53 Security and Privacy Controls for Information Systems and Organizations covers a broad range of technical considerations such as access control, incident response, system, and information integrity, and so on. The configuration management controls may provide useful guidance in the cryptographic discovery planning:

- Configuration management policy and procedures,
- Baseline configuration of the system,
- Configuration change control scope and procedures,

- Impact analysis of any proposed changes (e.g., post-quantum cryptography),
- Access restrictions for change,
- Configuration settings,
- Least functionality (e.g., close ports),
- System component inventory guidance,
- Configuration management plan,
- Software usage restrictions,
- User-installed software,
- Information location,
- Data action mapping,
- Signed components.

Later, as part of the risk analysis, organizations are advised to complete a comprehensive inventory of their cryptography, and reviewing this NIST controls document, like configuration management, will help the organization develop an inventory approach (also known as a cryptographic discovery audit) aligned with best practices, thereby improving quality, and reducing cryptography inventory risks. By understanding the scope and complexity of configuration management, the project manager and technology leadership are likely to craft realistic project plans to reach their target state.

Quantum Algorithms

Another valuable NIST project has been to evaluate post-quantum cryptographic algorithms. NIST is standardizing algorithms intended to protect systems and data against attacks using cryptographically-relevant quantum computers. They followed an iterative process to collect feedback about proposed algorithms and they have winnowed down the number of algorithms to the following:

1. CRYSTALS-Kyber for general encryption purposes such as creating secure websites,
2. CRYSTALS-Dilithium to protect the digital signatures for signing documents remotely,

3. SPHINCS+ designed for digital signatures,

4. FALCON also designed for digital signatures.

The organization's IT security and procurement strategy, policies, and procedures will likely be updated to reflect these new post-quantum-resistant algorithms and how they can be applied in a hybrid cryptographic environment. As these are first generation algorithms, they may require updates to improve their performance or to address vulnerabilities making cryptographic agility a high priority for organizations to maintain readiness.

Microlearning

The NIST Cybersecurity Framework is a *living* framework of best practices that will reward the learner with repeat visits to NIST websites:

- Review the NIST family of documents. There are links to these documents in our References appendix,
- Sign up for and search for NIST updates (e.g., C2M2 maturity model alignment with NIST or post-quantum cryptographic profile guidance),
- Identify the relevant cryptographic trends related to hybrid cryptographic environments and their implications for cryptographic migration projects,
- Use online tools to compare the NIST Cybersecurity Framework to the ISO/IEC 27001 ISM standard or the ISA/IEC 62443 series of standards for industrial automation and control systems security.

ISO/IEC 27000 Information Security Management

Another popular cybersecurity standard is the ISO/IEC 27000—ISM systems family of standards. Like the NIST Cybersecurity Framework, ISO manages a set of cybersecurity standards applicable to any industry, of any size (Figure 2.6).

There are three ISO ISM goals: achieve the right amount of (i) information availability, (ii) integrity, and (iii) confidentiality. The ISO

ISO/IEC 27000 *Overview*				
ISO/IEC 27003 *Implementation*	**ISO/IEC 27004** *Measurement*	**ISO/IEC 27005** *Risk*	**ISO/IEC 27007** *Auditing*	**ISO/IEC 27001** *Requirements*
ISO/IEC 27021 *Competence*	**ISO/IEC 27031** *Business Continuity*	**ISO/IEC 27035** *Incident Management*	**ISO/IEC 27036** *Suppliers*	**ISO/IEC 27002** *Code of Practice*

Figure 2.6 ISO/IEC security management family of standards (partial listing)

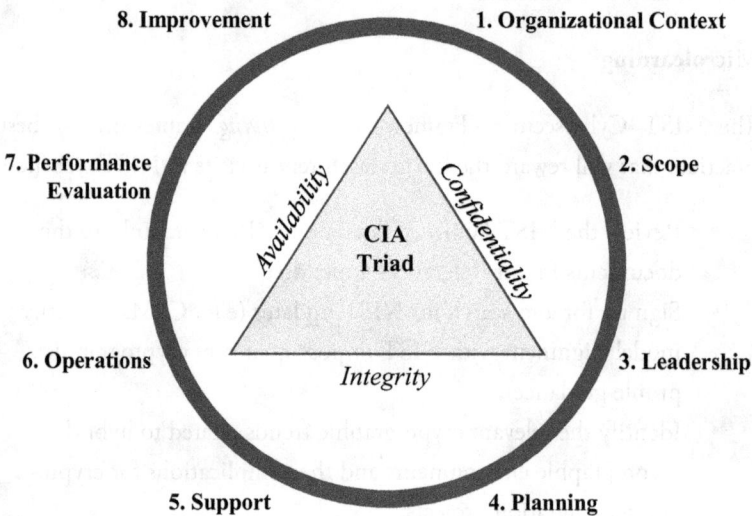

Figure 2.7 ISO/IEC 27000 compliance elements

family of cybersecurity standards focuses on this CIA Triad (Figure 2.7) and is also included in the ITIL ISM practice. Like the ITIL ISM practice and the NIST Cybersecurity Framework, the ISO/IEC 27000 series is process-based, holistic, and iterative with a core focus on risk management. These best practices are meant to be tailored and judiciously adopted forming a minimum viable cybersecurity framework.

A critical difference between the NIST Cybersecurity Framework and the ISO/IEC 27000 standards is an organization can become certified in the ISO/IEC 27000 family of standards. These certifications signify the organization's people, processes, and technologies follow best practices in information security. While the NIST Cybersecurity Framework includes an audit process and tiers to guide continual improvement, one does not get certified in the NIST Cybersecurity Framework. To get ISO/IEC 27000 certified, one goes through a certification process and provides evidence of information security best practices.

A program management approach can be implemented by organizations following ISO/IEC 27000 Information Security, Cybersecurity and Privacy Protection, NIST Cybersecurity Framework, or both approaches¶ since we are focused on quantum project and program management rather than cybersecurity minutia like technical controls. Any critical functional differences between the ISO/IEC 27000 series and the NIST Cybersecurity Framework can be elaborated in the project design phase. For example, a cybersecurity application might be configured to provide NIST-style reports using NIST terminology (e.g., gap analysis by NIST functions, categories, and subcategories).

Microlearning

While *Quantum Cybersecurity* uses the NIST Cybersecurity Framework to anchor cybersecurity project and program management, the ISO/IEC 27000 series is also popular:

- Search for which is preferential for your industry: NIST or ISO cybersecurity?
- How long does it take to get ISO/IEC 27000 certified?
- What regulatory frameworks apply to your industry that has security implications (e.g., data security)?

Project Management Frameworks

Cybersecurity projects, including post-quantum cryptographic migrations, can benefit from a hybrid project management approach,** that is, apply, tailor, and combine project management tools, techniques,

---

¶ Some organizations have an international presence and may comply with both the ISO/IEC 27000 family of standards and NIST Cybersecurity Framework.

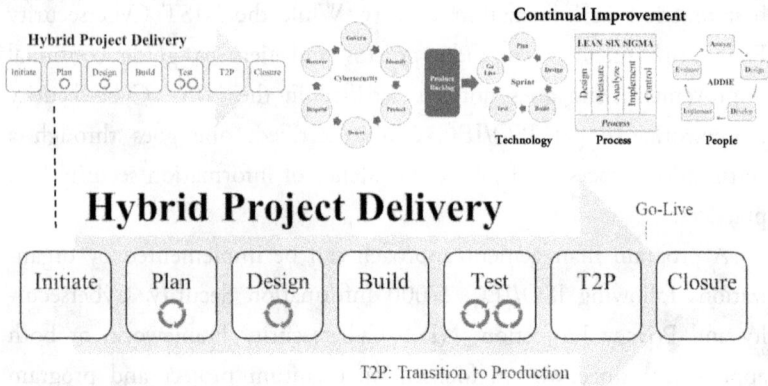

Figure 2.8 Hybrid project delivery approach

and processes from different project delivery approaches to cybersecurity projects to improve the probability of success. There is a continuum of project management approaches ranging from traditional to adaptive project delivery that can be combined and tailored precisely for quantum projects and initiatives.

Hybrid Project Management

The traditional or waterfall delivery approach is the oldest approach to delivering products and services with a long history of success (and failure when risk management is insufficient)! We build on this proven approach by tailoring and combining other standards and frameworks, arriving at a hybrid project management approach to implementing digital products and services like quantum technologies (Figure 2.8). Risk and quality management are prominent as they are in standards and frameworks. For example, there may be adaptive iterations in the project (e.g., problem-solving during proof-of-concept testing).

When technology is delivered, a transition to the production phase is included to prepare the new digital product (e.g., quantum-compliant APIs) or service (e.g., new software) for use in the production environment by the organization. The final tasks required to bring the digital products or services to the end users are critical, ranging from training the service desk team to completing the final technical

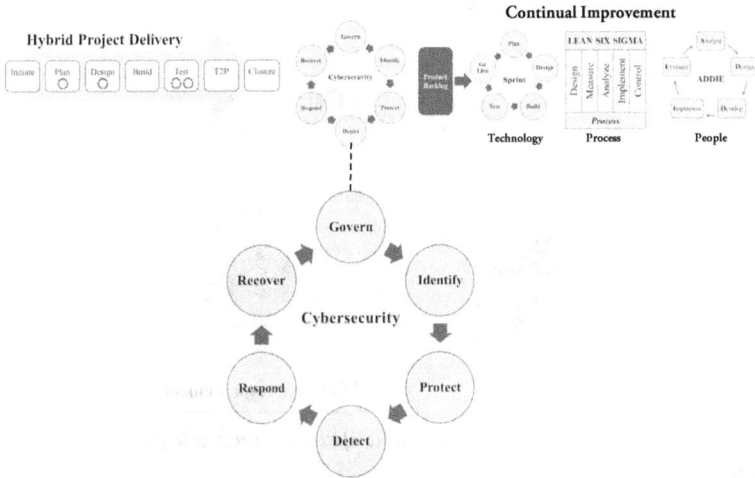

Figure 2.9 NIST *cybersecurity function*

tasks like quantum-resistant penetration testing. The project's product or service is handed over to the end user to derive value. In this book, we encourage a lean, hybrid project delivery approach, where *minimum viable products and services* or basic versions are provided to meet the basic minimum needs of the end users (also known as the *vanilla* or *Goldilocks*[††] version). After the technologies have been implemented and used, organizations can then collect optimization requests using the continual improvement of product backlog.

Organizations can use the hybrid project delivery approach to implement most cybersecurity software and other technologies most of the time (e.g., financial, healthcare, collaborative robotic manufacturing systems). Cybersecurity includes six functions from the NIST Cybersecurity Framework that are often delivered through projects and

---

[**] Hybrid project management is a delivery approach and is different from hybrid cryptography (e.g., layered cryptography with classical and post-quantum cryptographic algorithms), which is a technical approach to protecting data and systems.

[††] In a 19th-century fairy tale Goldilocks, the main character did not want too much, nor too little; Goldilocks always wanted just the right amount. Therefore, the *Goldilocks Principle* strives to apply not too much, nor too little cybersecurity, just the right amount to be successful. However, the moral of the *Goldilocks and the Three Bears* fairy tale is not to enter someone's home without their permission.

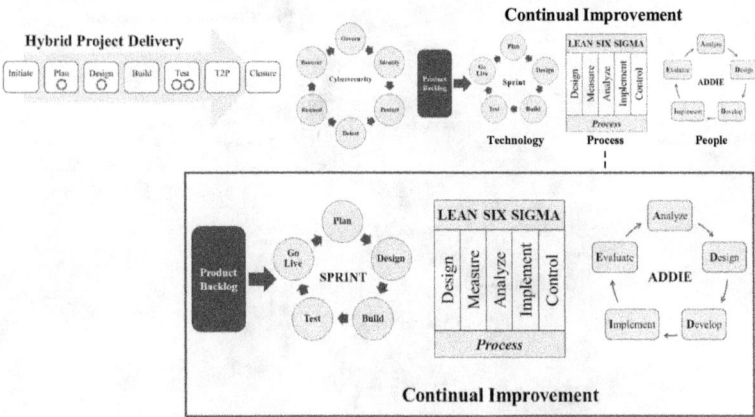

Figure 2.10 Continual improvement sprints—technology, process, and people

initiatives: govern, identify, protect, detect, respond, and recover (Figure 2.9).

In *Quantum Cybersecurity*, we combine continual improvement (ISO 9001) best practices with the NIST cybersecurity functions. Continual improvement is the process of planning, implementing, monitoring, and correcting any defects (or taking proactive action to improve cybersecurity readiness). It also includes periodic and formal reviews of external best practices. The IT security team applies these functions in the production environment (also known as the operational or live environment). They use cybersecurity software and may request new functionality or optimizations to improve their cybersecurity capabilities. These requests may be managed, prioritized, and approved through the ITIL Service Request Management practice. Once approved, the new functionality is scheduled for implementation through a significant project (Figure 2.8) or a smaller optimization sprint or initiative (Figure 2.10). Post-quantum migration and quantum agility projects can follow this approval process to improve quality and reduce risks—ITIL's value proposition.

There is no effective cybersecurity without a program of well-managed projects and initiatives; organizations cannot buy cybersecurity at their favorite online retailer or corner store. Therefore, project management is critical to cybersecurity readiness. While hybrid project management is a proven method to deliver most cybersecurity projects, some quantum technology projects can benefit from adaptive project management approaches like agile project management.

Adaptive Delivery Approaches

Adaptive project delivery approaches (agile, Lean Six Sigma, Kanban, etc.) have gained popularity and are increasingly used by project-oriented teams. When there is change and ambiguity, adaptive project delivery approaches can improve the probability of project success. In *Quantum Cybersecurity*, we recommend adaptive continual improvement approaches to optimize digital products and services like post-quantum cryptographic migrations, process improvement, and quantum skills training (Figure 2.10).

Organizations can use the hybrid project management delivery approach to deliver their minimum viable cybersecurity product or service. The IT security team uses the product backlog to prioritize and manage requests like adding new functionality or implementing post-quantum cryptographic migrations. Practitioners may use adaptive delivery approaches to optimize cybersecurity: agile project management (technologies), Lean Six Sigma (processes), and the ADDIE (Analyze, Design, Develop, Implement, and Evaluate) Model of Instructional Design (people—upskilling).

Agile Project Management: Technology

After cybersecurity (or any other technology) has been implemented, end users often request improvements or enhancements. For example, an IT cybersecurity supervisor may request a technology enhancement to activate additional IoT (Internet of Things) threat detection capabilities in their commercial cybersecurity software. Traditionally, large-scale improvements can be delivered with the hybrid project management approach (Figure 2.8), while minor technical optimizations (initiatives) can be implemented through adaptive delivery sprints (Figure 2.11). Additionally, when recurring projects become more routine (e.g., low ambiguity), many can be implemented as sprints (e.g., initiatives) that require less governance and documentation. For example, once the post-quantum cryptographic migration process completes the proof-of-concept, supported with training, templates, and checklists, subsequent migrations can be delegated to less experienced cybersecurity team members, while more senior staff work on complex and novel cybersecurity projects yet are available when support is required.

However, since quantum technologies are nascent and emerging, quantum subject matter experts (SMEs) do not always succeed with their technical plans and development; they try something else until they progress. Adaptive project delivery approaches like agile scrums are also helpful when the requirements are ambiguous, or the process or technology to deliver the product or service is ambiguous. Rather than planning the entire project with the hybrid project management approach, project managers break down the project and may plan month-long agile sprints using the product backlog (Figure 2.11). Therefore, many quantum research, development, and implementation projects can benefit from an agile approach when problem-solving iterations are a natural way to progress.

Teams can use agile scrums (Figure 2.11) to optimize quantum technologies including cybersecurity. Agile project delivery is a common approach to continual improvement once the technology

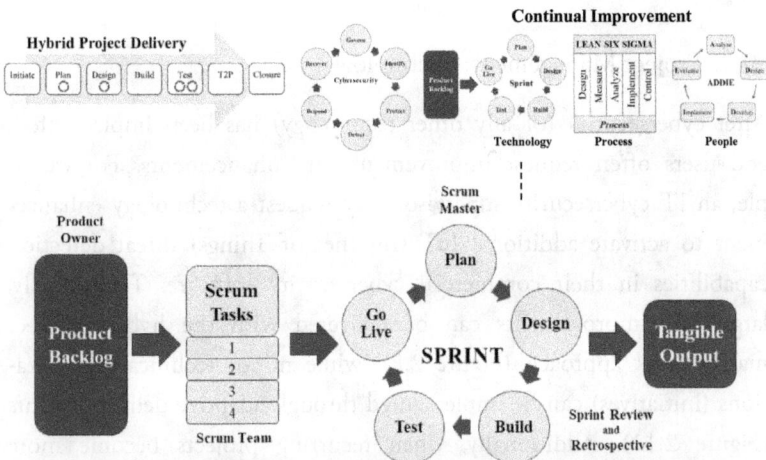

Figure 2.11 Adaptive project delivery approach—technology

is implemented and used (e.g., algorithmic rectification updates). Lessons learned activities (sprint review and retrospective) are part of agile sprints. There are numerous online resources about agile project management (e.g., Schwaber and Sutherland, 2017), the reader may review and tailor for their own projects and initiatives.

Microlearning

Increasingly, adaptive project delivery methods are used, resulting in many online resources:

- How did early space exploration use adaptive approaches to develop, test, and apply new technologies to fly to the moon? How does NASA use adaptive approaches?
- Search for which is better: agile or hybrid project management?
- When should agile project management be avoided? What are the main risks with an agile approach?
- What is the most surprising application of agile? For example, how is agile project management used in the museum industry?
- Why is following the Agile Manifesto a critical success factor for agile projects?

Lean Six Sigma: Process

Technology and IT security teams might use the Lean Six Sigma approach (Figure 2.12) to streamline and automate the post-quantum cryptographic migration process or ITIL processes (e.g., release management). The Lean Six Sigma approach brings together lean and the Six Sigma problem-solving approaches to improve process performance (e.g., throughput) by reducing or eliminating waste (Lean) and reducing process variation (Six Sigma).

Many digital transformation projects have process improvement goals, and the Lean Six Sigma results can be helpful during the design phase to transform bloated processes. The Lean Six Sigma problem-solving approach is process-based: define the project, measure to create a baseline, analyze the problem, improve by implementing the solution, and monitor and control the process to determine if waste and process

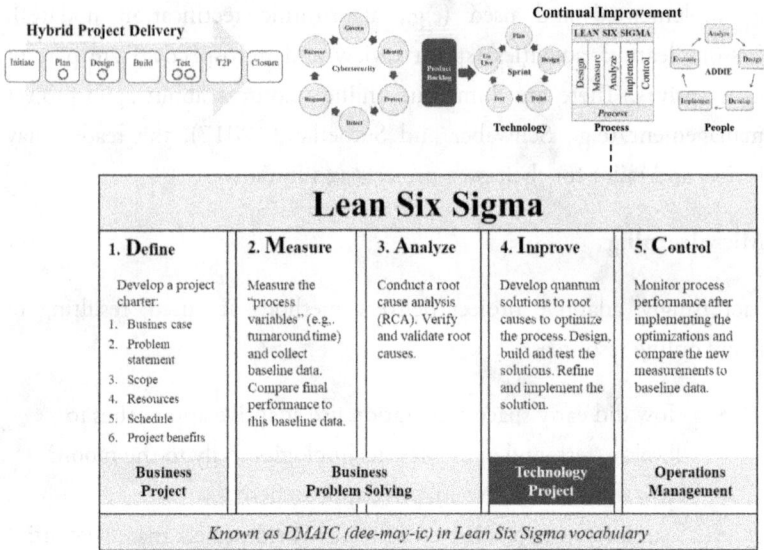

Figure 2.12 Lean Six Sigma—process

variation are reduced. At its core, Lean Six Sigma is about process optimization. Organizations may optimize and automate processes (e.g., change management approval workflows) before a sustained implementation of technologies like cryptographic migrations.

Business units (e.g., pharmacy operations, engineering, accounts payable, manufacturing) often develop strategic plans to improve their processes and quantum workflow optimization can trigger Lean Six Sigma projects. In the Lean Six Sigma *improve* phase, business partners may request technology to automate or optimize steps in their value-creation processes. Therefore, their process improvement project (Figure 2.12) may require a quantum technology project to optimize their workflow (e.g., speeding up and automating steps in the process) and be implemented during the DMAIC improve phase. Practitioners can follow the hybrid project management approach (tailoring and combining) to provide DMAIC-based improvements. New processes often require new training in the process or supporting technologies requests, which can be prioritized and added to the product backlog.

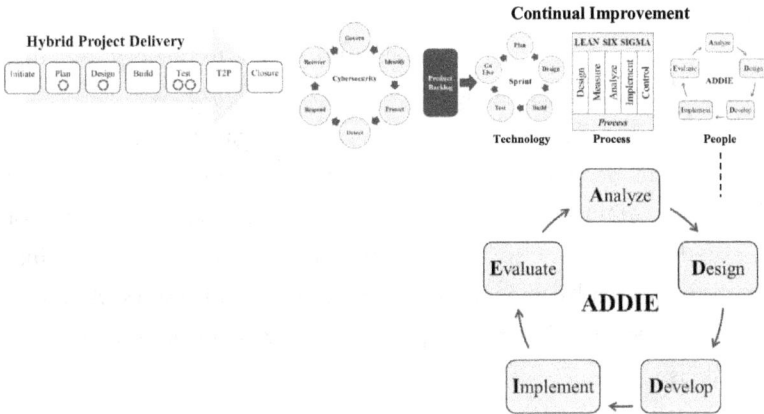

Figure 2.13 ADDIE model of instructional design—people

Microlearning

The Lean Six Sigma problem-solving approach is used to improve processes (e.g., reduced turn-around-time) including those in the IT department, PMO, and security units. There are many online resources, including free Lean Six Sigma training:

- What are Lean Six Sigma best practices?
- What are Lean Six Sigma implementation risks?
- Can you find Lean Six Sigma quantum use cases and success stories?
- What Lean Six Sigma tools and templates are available for post-quantum cryptographic migrations?

ADDIE Model of Instructional Design: People

Organizations can use ADDIE sprints to improve an organization's people capabilities in the quantum ecosystem (Figure 2.13). The ADDIE model of instructional design can be tailored to develop training programs aligned to ITIL technology project management.[‡‡]

[‡‡] Greg Skulmoski and Chris Walker wrote *Cybersecurity Training: A Pathway to Readiness* (2023) and detailed how to plan, deliver, and optimize cybersecurity training and learning by aligning with best practices including the ADDIE

The ADDIE model is used worldwide and is the gold standard for training and applies well to cybersecurity and technology training, including quantum upskilling.

Given the shortage of quantum skills, organizations will likely nurture and develop some of their own quantum experts and may follow the ADDIE model of instructional design. However, many of the desired quantum skills are commonly developed in engineering, mathematics, and computer science faculties at universities. Adopting quantum technologies including cybersecurity requires new job roles and skills:

- Quantum business analysts develop ways to apply quantum technologies to the organization's processes such as in supply chain optimization and management,
- Quantum policy and ethics analysts guide the organization to apply quantum technologies ethically,
- Quantum software engineers create algorithms and program software to apply quantum technologies to problems and opportunities such as schedule and budget management in the project management office,
- Quantum hardware engineers design, build, maintain, and upgrade the hardware in the quantum ecosystem,
- Quantum project managers initiate, plan, design, build, test, implement, stabilize, and close out quantum technology projects (people, process, and technology),
- Quantum educators follow the ADDIE model of instructional design to analyze quantum-related training requirements, design and develop materials, and implement and evaluate quantum-related training and learning,
- Quantum sales and marketing specialists market and sell the quantum products and services generated by the organization.

Quantum SMEs, including post-quantum cryptographic migration specialists, are in short supply and organizations are advised to find

model of instructional design, Bloom's taxonomy of cognitive thought, and the Kirkpatrick model of evaluation.

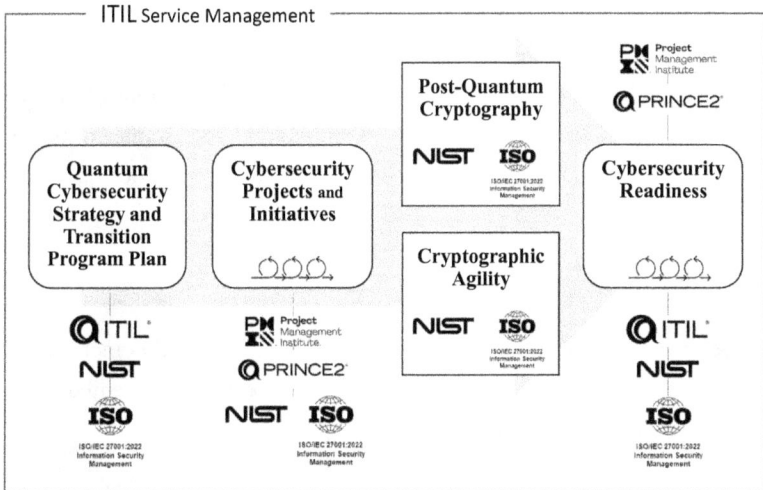

Figure 2.14 Quantum-aligned cybersecurity standards and frameworks

ways to optimize their capabilities. With a combination of upskilling and pushing less complex cybersecurity projects to others, organizations can optimize their quantum and other talent while balancing work–life realities.

Thus, organizations can implement initiatives (e.g., to optimize processes, upskill people), and implement technologies with adaptive project delivery techniques including using the product backlog. Product backlogs can be heterogeneous and include continual improvement requests (Figure 2.10). The product backlog includes technical initiatives like adding new integration (agile sprints), removing *pain points* from a process through automation (process improvement), or providing new cybersecurity training (ADDIE model). The product backlog may include classical computing and quantum technology sprints. Therefore, the overall product backlog will have a mix of prioritized initiatives to optimize the digital product or service.

Organizations can adopt, tailor, and combine best practices found in standards and frameworks for their projects and initiatives like migrating to post-quantum cryptography or optimizing cryptographic agility (Figure 2.14).

Quantum Cybersecurity Program Management is based on best practices found in global de facto standards and frameworks. The value proposition in these best practices promises the right amount of quality and reduced risks. Best practices in standards and frameworks are applied, tailored, and combined to support a lean program of quantum projects and initiatives.

Microlearning

Cybersecurity training is a growing field because of the increase in cybersecurity incidents involving people that can be prevented with competent and cyber-savvy people:

- Search for the minimum viable competencies organizations require for a quantum ecosystem,
- Find case studies of the ADDIE model used in quantum technology training.

CHAPTER 3

Quantum
Transition Strategies

> *Strategy is not a single process that starts at one point and ends neatly at another. Defining, planning, and implementing a strategy are cyclical activities, which are performed in multiple areas of the organization at any time. Strategy is a formal, defined set of activities that follow the continual improvement model* (Axelos 2020, 35).

In Chapter 3, we combine IT strategy, quantum cybersecurity, project management, and service management best practices found in standards and frameworks to provide strategies for a transition to quantum readiness. The World Economic Forum (2022a, 42) recommends that organizations develop quantum technology service management strategies: "More businesses need to understand the implications of quantum computing on their industry and formulate a quantum computing strategy." Therefore, we present a three-pronged strategic approach leveraging the ITIL Strategic Management practice to transition to a secure quantum environment (Figure 3.1):

1. **Quantum business strategy:** Develop business cases based on quantum technologies to advance the organizations' business strategy. Organizations improve the probability of success when strategies are developed, implemented, and monitored (and controlled if necessary) using best practices like those found in ITIL or Control Objectives for Information and Related Technologies (COBIT) service management.

2. **Quantum technology strategy:** Develop a technology strategy that supports the quantum business strategy and transitions

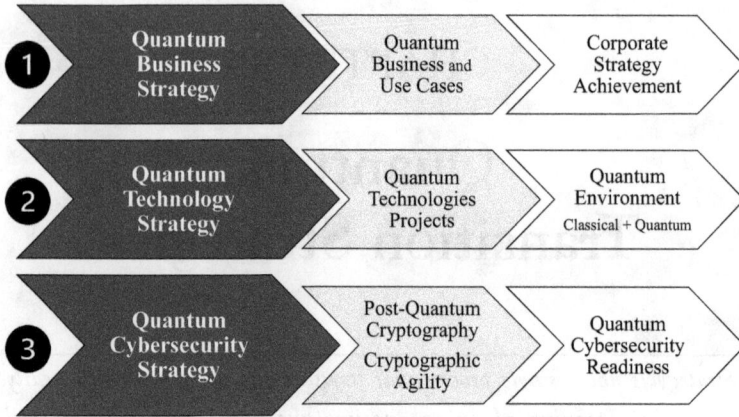

Figure 3.1 Quantum transition strategies

the organization from its classical computing environment to a hybrid environment of classical and quantum computing technologies and beyond. Organizations can benefit from developing a quantum technology strategy again by following ITIL or COBIT service management since providing quantum technologies is a service like other technologies.

3. **Quantum cybersecurity strategy:** Develop a quantum cybersecurity strategy to protect not only existing but future digital assets and information. Once a minimum viable cybersecurity foundation is established, the organization can begin initiating post-quantum cryptographic migrations and cryptographic agility projects and initiatives.

Organizations can craft a holistic quantum strategy by first developing a business strategy. To develop the quantum business strategy (as well as the quantum technology and cybersecurity strategies), organizations can follow, and tailor digital service management best practices found in either ITIL or COBIT frameworks. The importance of applying formal methods to transition to quantum technologies is supported by other quantum insiders. We align, combine, and tailor the best practices within ITIL service management and the PMBOK® Guide to direct our quantum projects.

The purpose of a strategy is to guide organizational action to achieve its vision, goals, and objectives through a program of projects and initiatives. A strategy is like a lighthouse in stormy weather to guide the ship's crew to safety; quality is improved, and risks are reduced. There are many benefits to developing, implementing, and governing strategies like increased operational resilience, efficiency, and effectiveness; enhanced sense of purpose for stakeholders; and improved risk management. However, there are related risks to strategy such as it can be time-consuming and difficult to apply without a comprehensive delivery approach (e.g., project and service management). We leave it to the reader to find out more about strategy development while we provide an overview of strategies as they pertain to quantum technologies.

Quantum Business Strategy

A transition to quantum technologies and applications for a business unit or organization begins with a cohesive quantum business strategy. Being among the first to adopt new technologies like quantum computing is a classical industry disruption strategy that can improve the organization's ability to compete and deliver value (AXELOS 2020, 40). Some organizations follow maturity models to grow their strategies as they adopt quantum technologies and apply them to business use cases (AXELOS 2020, 45).

Fundamental to a business strategy is the vision, a quantum technologies vision. "The organization will need to move from its current way of working and institute new processes, practices, systems, and skills. It can be a daunting undertaking, and a clear digital vision can overcome fears and drive positive action" (AXELOS 2020, 49). Therefore, an early task in a quantum journey is to develop a quantum-inspired business vision.

Quantum-Inspired Business Vision

Quantum technologies can make the impossible possible and provide new opportunities for innovators. Therefore, organizations may revisit their organizational vision and tune it to leverage quantum technologies. Working through the intricacies of drafting an organization's vision is out of scope for *Quantum Cybersecurity* and in the purview of MBA studies and consultancy; however, we do offer a few guidelines, best practices, and examples.

What is a quantum vision? A vision is the organization's aspiration of what it will become, its future, or its target state. Therefore, a quantum vision describes a future organization serviced with quantum technologies. That quantum future may be better, faster, cheaper, or transformative to something entirely new for the organization. Updating the organization's vision for the quantum era is a critical success factor for digital transformation success. Here are some industry-specific examples of quantum-inspired vision statements:

Healthcare data management: to harden data security and encryption with post-quantum cryptographically secure technologies, guaranteeing the availability, confidentiality, and integrity of our client's sensitive and critical healthcare information.

Communications technologies: to unlock and accelerate the full potential of free-space quantum research and development, providing new technologies for defense-oriented satellites and drones.

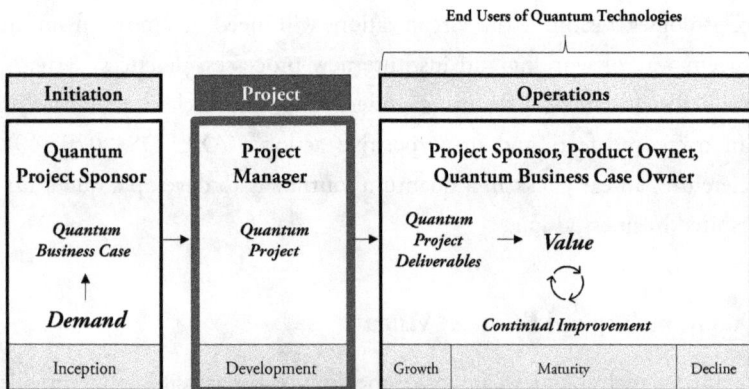

Figure 3.2 Quantum product or service lifecycle

Financial services: to revolutionize wealth and risk management with quantum technologies, providing high-value clients with precision investments despite uncertain markets.

Architecture: to disrupt the architecture design industry with quantum-generated digital twins providing unrivaled simulations and feasible designs.

The organization's quantum vision statement will drive technology and cybersecurity strategy and projects. Consider reviewing your organization's or department's current vision statement with your team to envision a quantum-enabled future (e.g., the classical gap analysis approach). The NIST Cybersecurity Framework provides a similar approach to visioning and guides the organization to understand both the current and target (future) states, then implement projects and initiatives to address any gaps. The ADKAR (Awareness, Desire, Knowledge, Ability, and Reinforcement) change management approach also has gap analysis techniques (e.g., change and readiness evaluations).

The vision can be supplemented with the quantum use case. For example, the organization may wish to adopt quantum technologies (e.g., combinatorial optimization) in its supply chain and include use case objectives regarding its people, processes, and technologies (sometimes referred to as the three pillars of IT):

Objective 1—process: Streamline the supply chain inventory management processes with quantum-enabled AI forecasting.

Objective 2—technology: Implement quantum technologies to predict demand for supplies to optimize inventory availability, minimize costs, and maximize inventory turnover.

Objective 3—people: Hire quantum programming and modeling personnel and upskill supply chain team members in applying quantum technologies.

Developing a business strategy, vision, and objectives to adopt quantum technologies aligns with ITIL service management best practices and expects iterative collaboration between business units and

IT leadership. We leave it to the reader to investigate quantum business strategies while we focus on program management.

Microlearning

There is a large body of knowledge online about developing a business-driven technology strategy, vision, and objectives:

- Find examples of earlier industry disruptions due to new technologies, risks encountered, and their lessons learned as you contemplate your quantum journey,
- Learn about guidelines and best practices for developing a quantum vision statement,
- Generate sample vision statements, strategies, and objectives for your industry and target state,
- How are quantum vision workshops structured? What are workshop best practices?

Quantum Business Case

A practical way to achieve organizational objectives supporting a quantum vision is to develop business cases within ITIL's service management approach. The quantum business use case reflects the *demand* in the ITIL Service Value System (Figure 2.1). While we provide an overview, readers unfamiliar with developing a business case leveraging quantum technologies may consult other resources. A quantum business case starts the quantum product or service lifecycle (Figure 3.2). If the business case is sufficiently large, it may be implemented as a program or portfolio. In *Quantum Cybersecurity Program Management,* we briefly introduce the quantum business case and its application.

Business cases are standard tools in product and service management; business cases outline and quantify the innovation or opportunity. Organizations develop business cases to analyze potential opportunities in terms of whether they align with an organization's strategic goals, the level of demand for the quantum-enabled product or service, and their competitors among other analyses. Developing a business case can be

Table 3.1 Quantum business case elements

Business case name and description	Select a name for the quantum business case that will be appropriate throughout the entire product or service lifecycle and briefly describe the main points,
Product/service manager (project sponsor)	Identify the product/service manager who owns the quantum business case and will be responsible for the product or service and generating value. This role is the service owner in the ITIL Framework,
Organizational strategy alignment	Describe how the proposed business case is aligned with organizational strategy and objectives. (e.g., How does workflow optimization contribute to business strategy?),
Other options considered	Provide an overview of other business cases that were considered (e.g., classical and quantum technologies),
External analysis	Analyze the current and future market opportunities, competitive analysis, risk versus reward, and so on,
Product/service benefits	Describe the benefits of the proposed quantum business case to the organization and stakeholders including any sustainable development goals (GPM 2023, 64),
Product/service timelines	Provide a high-level Gantt chart (bar chart schedule) of the quantum product/service lifecycle: (i) inception, (ii) development, (iii) growth, (iv) maturity, and (v) decline,
Costs	Evaluate the *make/buy* decision regarding how quantum technologies may be introduced to the organization and estimate product/service lifecycle costs aligned with their timelines,
Return on investment	Calculate the return on investment for the proposed quantum business case; finance teams can assist,
Risks and issues	Identify the key risks and issues for each phase of the quantum product or service lifecycle,
Recommendations and next steps	Include what should be done and the immediate actions to advance the recommendations.

assisted with online tools (Table 3.1, developed from multiple online resources like *How to Write a Business Case*).

The goal is to demonstrate a clear alignment between business case and organizational vision, goals, and objectives. To develop a quantum business case, the product owner follows best practices and conducts external and internal analyses (AXELOS 2020, 54). Developing an understanding of the internal and external environments (and the interplay between them), improves the quality of the quantum business case.

While these are common business case elements, again we encourage the reader to tailor and combine as necessary to arrive at minimum viable quantum business cases. There are risks related to not following a structured approach to adopting quantum technologies including post-quantum cryptography projects and initiatives:

> Many organizations have plunged into digital transformation initiatives without knowing whether they had the appropriate capabilities and practices. Unfortunately, few organizations know where to begin or what it takes to prepare for digital transformation; as a result, few initiatives are successful" (AXELOS 2020, 61).

Transitioning to a quantum ecosystem is a digital transformation program of such complexity and criticality few have seen before. Therefore, in *Quantum Cybersecurity*, we recommend a formal approach to developing a quantum business case as outlined in the *ITIL 4: Digital and IT Strategy* practice (Axelos 2020) or in business strategy development guides. Some begin their quantum business case analysis by examining the external and internal environments to identify gaps, risks, and opportunities.

External Analysis

The quantum service owner will examine the external environment (e.g., environmental analysis) to evaluate changes in their market and industry with the goal to adapt, flourish, and perhaps disrupt. A popular environmental analysis approach for a proposed quantum business case is PESTLE: analyze the politics, economics, social factors, technology, legal issues, and the environment. There are other external environmental analysis techniques that can benefit a quantum business case such as strengths, weaknesses, opportunities, and threats (SWOT), scenario analysis, value ecosystem mapping, competitor analysis, Porter's five forces analysis, and so on. Organizations will closely consider their supply chain as the members will need to transition to post-quantum cryptography, or the organization may need to find another partner(s). The quantum service owner will also monitor external milestones like error correction progress to determine the arrival timing of a crypto-graphically-relevant quantum computer.

Internal Analysis

The ITIL Framework outlines dimensions of digital service management that guide quantum business case development (Table 3.2). Should any of the dimensions be weak, then a dimension gap needs to be addressed to improve the probability of implementing a successful business use case (AXELOS 2020, 57).

With a holistic approach (people, process, and technology) to business case development and analysis, there is a greater probability of successful quantum projects.

Organizational Quantum Readiness Gap Analysis

The results of the external and internal analyses are combined and further analyzed, and any quantum business strategy gaps are prioritized

Table 3.2 Dimensions affecting a quantum business case

Dimension	Readiness Analysis
People	Internal: the organization's structures, people, competencies, leadership, culture, role clarity, collaboration capabilities and so on related to the quantum business case
	External: the quantum ecosystem that allows partners and suppliers to provide goods and services to the organization that are valued
Process	Internal and external: the end-to-end value stream of activities, processes, steps, procedures, and workflows used to deliver quantum-related products and services. The Lean Six Sigma problem-solving approach can be used to optimize value streams and processes for emerging technologies
Technology	Internal and external: the information and technology ecosystems to support the quantum business use case are analyzed to determine if there are technology gaps (e.g., analyze the organization's current and target states)

for action. The ITIL approach (AXELOS 2020, 57) provides gap analysis guidance, for example:

- What level of organizational maturity is required to implement the quantum business case?
- What are common constraints and assumptions when implementing a quantum business case?
- What quantum-related competencies (e.g., knowledge, skills, experience) are required?
- What are the unique features of the organization that distinguish it from competitors that can be leveraged with quantum technologies?
- Is re-organizing the business structure required to optimize the quantum business strategy?
- Which quantum technologies are required and in what sequence?

Organizations address environmental gaps (internal and external) through larger strategic projects and smaller initiatives, as well as through partnerships and collaborations. They initiate projects (e.g., minimum viable foundation projects) to close gaps to improve the probability of a successful quantum business strategy. Like any work breakdown structure, there are many ways to elaborate scope such as by quantum objectives (Figure 3.3). By categorizing the gaps (e.g., technology) and framing the analysis in ITIL terminology, a holistic understanding of the quantum vision is more likely.

Therefore, a visual and categorized representation of gaps can improve the reader's understanding of the quantum program of projects to achieve the business strategy.

To summarize thus far, objectives are designed to achieve the organization's vision, and the gap analysis represents deficiencies or bottlenecks to achieving the objectives and vision. Projects and initiatives deliver capabilities to close gaps and remove bottlenecks, and organizational objectives and its vision are more likely to be achieved.

The transition to quantum technologies gap analysis can reported and prioritized for action (AXELOS 2020, 62):

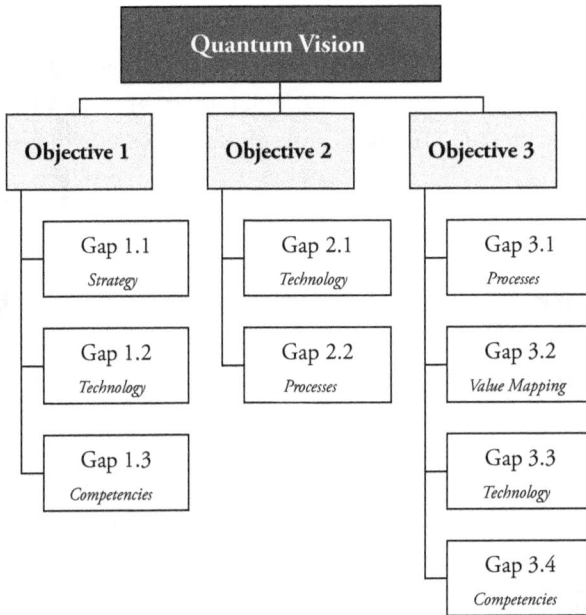

Figure 3.3 Gap analysis linked to quantum objectives

Gap analysis overview and objectives: Provide an overview of the gap analysis process (to provide the message: *good process, good result*) and its objectives (e.g., future or target state to achieve quantum readiness).

Current state overview and gaps: Identify and prioritize the gaps that prevent the organization from reaching each quantum objective and outline what is required (e.g., people, process, and technology) to reach the future state and close the gaps (Figures 2.5 and 3.3).

Future state actions: Identify, prioritize, approve, and implement a program of projects and initiatives to close gaps, remove bottlenecks, and achieve the future quantum state—the focus of this book.

If not already, quantum champions from the business side of the organization will want to collaborate with technology leadership to implement their quantum vision and quantum use cases. They may invite technology leadership to business visioning exercises and during the CapEx (Capital Expenditure) and OpEx (Operating Expenditure) budgeting cycles used to fund major projects. When businesses provide their IT partners with a concise quantum business strategy and use cases and aligned with the ITIL, the quantum collaboration can flourish.

Microlearning

Organizations develop and approve business cases, implement projects, and deliver innovative products and services (e.g., project deliverables). Business faculties offer popular courses in business case development, and as such, you can find copious information online to guide your quantum business case development:

- Discover the diversity of business cases and styles, and look for an approach that fits your organization (e.g., a materials simulation quantum business case will be different than a financial optimization quantum business case),
- Look for processes and tools to evaluate a business opportunity, including quantum-business cases investment prioritization and analysis,
- Find quantum business cases to optimize the CapEx/OpEx approval cycle,
- Find ADKAR change management tools, processes, and techniques applicable to quantum projects,
- Generate an environmental analysis for your proposed quantum business use case using the PESTLE approach combined with other methods like scenario, SWOT, or option space analysis; value ecosystem mapping; competitor analysis; and so on.

Quantum Technology Strategy

The quantum business strategy, business case, and objectives drive the quantum technology strategy, and the quantum technology strategy drives the quantum cybersecurity strategy. Therefore, IT leadership and their team look for a cohesive business strategy as an input to their strategic planning to adopt quantum technologies and transition to quantum readiness (Figures 2.14 and 3.1).

Start With a Quantum Technology Vision

Developing or revising the quantum technology vision may begin with reviewing the quantum business strategy to understand end-user expectations (e.g., the demand for quantum technology services). While business units develop quantum business use cases, the supporting technology needs to be provided either internally or externally (e.g., quantum applications as a service). The IT and security architects will design a minimum viable quantum architecture tailored to the organization. Stakeholder expectations may need to be tempered since project timelines may be long should the gap analysis reveal significant work is required to support the business case (e.g., deliver new technologies and integration to close gaps prior to implementing quantum technologies). In the interim, business stakeholders can improve their quantum skill sets and perhaps access a quantum *sandbox* (also known as a *playground*) to explore and experiment with quantum capabilities.

Quantum Technologies Strategy: What and How

The quantum technology strategy answers the questions: "what is our target technology profile and how do we get there?" In *Quantum Cybersecurity*, we include transitioning to post-quantum cryptography agility. We briefly address implementing quantum technologies and use cases where the resulting projects may occur concurrently with the organization's quantum cybersecurity projects. When faced with the make-buy decision, we assume that most quantum technology adopters will start their journey with Quantum-as-a-Service (QaaS) from one of the major technology providers as building is cost prohibitive for most. We leave such financial and strategic analysis for other thought leaders to address while we focus on quantum program management.

Current State Risk Identification and Analysis

In the ITIL approach to technology management, a *digital readiness assessment* is one of the early actions required—indeed a critical success factor—for a minimum viable foundation of quantum technologies to enable business use cases (AXELOS 2020, 61) and new technologies to support post-quantum cryptographic migrations and cryptographic agility. The purpose of analyzing where we are today is like creating a baseline to understand risks and opportunities. Analyzing digital readiness is appropriate when use case criticality and complexity are high, as in quantum technologies and post-quantum cryptographic migrations. Digital readiness assessments reveal deficiencies and perhaps opportunities that allow the organization to pinpoint where to invest resources. Identifying deficiencies is part of the process to reach the desired future state (e.g., post-quantum cryptography agility).

ITIL's digital readiness assessment aligns with the NIST Cybersecurity Framework's *current profile* of what is currently being provided and achieved. NIST Cybersecurity Framework users are also guided to create or review the current profile when establishing or improving a cybersecurity program. If the organization's external network is significant, the organization may develop a community profile of its current state (NIST 2024, 6). Both NIST and ITIL recommend conducting a gap analysis between the organization's current and future states. Therefore, if the reader desires more guidance than is in the NIST Cybersecurity Framework, they can refer to the ITIL's digital readiness assessment (AXELOS 2020, 61).

One can determine the current profile of the organization's capabilities with a lean quantum readiness assessment based on the ITIL approach (ITIL 2022, 61) in Table 3.3.

The reader is invited to conduct further analysis in each capability category. For example, the assessment team may identify and analyze the organization's most used processes to approve, release, and optimize technology services; these processes may be tuned to support lean post-quantum cryptographic migrations. Often, the benefit from this exercise is not determining the rating; rather, it is understanding

Table 3.3 Assessing quantum digital readiness

Technical Capability	Digital Readiness Rating
Strategy and digital positioning: the degree to which the quantum transition vision, benefits, and execution are shared across the organization	Low–medium–high
Governance: the maturity and capabilities of:	
1. IT roles, responsibilities, policies, processes, and procedures related to quantum technologies	Low–medium–high
2. Quantum program management, including initiating, planning, monitoring, controlling, and reporting progress	Low–medium–high
Practices and processes: the degree to which the organization's practices and processes support the quantum vision and objectives	Low–medium–high
Value streams: the degree to which the organization's quantum-related value streams are understood and mapped	Low–medium–high
Information and technology: the degree to which the organization's digital ecosystem can be transitioned to quantum technologies to improve the customer experience and/or operational excellence	Low–medium–high
Supply chain information and technology: the degree the organization's supply chain stakeholders' digital ecosystem can be transitioned to quantum technologies	Low–medium–high
Organizational development and learning: the degree the organization's people and partners can plan, implement, operate, maintain, and optimize the quantum ecosystem	Low–medium–high
Risk management: the degree the organization balances digital risks and rewards throughout the product or service lifecycle including enterprise risk management	Low–medium–high
Innovation: the degree digital innovations like quantum technologies are supported and integrated in the organization	Low–medium–high

the variances of stakeholder opinions and discussing why the organization may or may not be ready to transition to a quantum ecosystem. Thus, the team can develop a shared understanding of an organization's quantum capabilities by discussing the digital readiness rating variances and where agreement is realized, then plan and prioritize for action.

While the project team begins by analyzing the current technical state, it is common in IT projects that new technology requires supporting capabilities like upskilled people, updated value stream processes, policies, procedures, and so on. Therefore, it is prudent to extend the quantum readiness assessment beyond technology as other supporting capabilities (as seen in Table 3.3) may need to be in place for the organization to succeed with quantum technologies and business use cases.

The output of the quantum readiness assessment reveals risks and opportunities, or SWOT, and the gaps between the target and current states. The organization then develops a holistic technology strategy (people, process, and technology), to reach the target technology ecosystem. The project manager and teams implement these strategies through projects and initiatives.

Target State Identification—An Agile Quantum Ecosystem

Organizations identify the target state (future profile) by documenting the vision, general goals, and specific objectives. Documenting the target state in the IT strategy is carefully completed as it will guide the organization and project teams to implement a sustained program of projects. An early task in strategy formulation is to conduct a quantum technologies gap analysis.

Quantum Technologies Gap Analysis

The digital readiness assessment of their current state reveals the organization's gaps, strengths, and weaknesses in their transition to quantum technologies (see also Table 3.3 and Figure 3.3). The gap analyses are inputs into the quantum technology and cybersecurity strategies to guide future projects and initiatives that are planned, implemented, used, and later improved (ITIL Service Value System, Figure 2.1). The technical and security architects and key planners take a holistic approach and consider people and processes when planning and prioritizing projects to incrementally move to the technology target state; implementing technologies without people committed to, skilled in, and engaged with quantum technologies will result in feeble technology adoption.

Organizations may implement no-regret projects where the initial quantum projects build a platform to allow future development and agility regardless the technological pathway that unfolds. For example, the organization may strengthen testing by aligning with ITIL's Service Validation and Testing practice and providing testing templates and checklists to improve testing quality and reduce testing risks for the decade of quantum projects to come.

Hybrid State

Transitioning to quantum technologies may include a hybrid state with a combination of high-performance, classical, and quantum computing components. For example, we may continue to develop business presentations with classical computers and software, while using high-performance computers with quantum technologies to run manufacturing optimization simulations. Performance-intensive computing (PIC), also known as high-performance computing (HPC), focuses on maximizing computational power to tackle complex problems that require significant classical computing capabilities. It typically involves supercomputers, high-performance clusters, and specialized hardware to perform tasks that would be impractical or extremely time-consuming on standard computing platforms. These HPC systems can be enhanced with quantum computing processors and supporting technologies (e.g., new interfaces).

The organization's technology strategy may detail how to adopt quantum technologies: (i) implement quantum technologies in-house (e.g., on-site or on-premises) or (ii) through a cloud-based subscription from a vendor (e.g., QaaS). Some industries like defense, finance, and healthcare may prefer in-house installations for improved security or regulatory requirements. Therefore, the quantum technology strategy includes a holistic approach to move from classical to mixed computing technologies to advance the organization's vision, goals, and objectives.

Minimum Viable Projects

Minimum viable projects and initiatives address technology or cybersecurity gaps. These projects represent meeting regulatory thresholds or minimum viable foundations to build future innovations or leverage intended capabilities. For example, technology gaps may prevent an organization from implementing the *Essential Eight* cybersecurity strategies (Australian Signals Directorate 2022). The organization may implement a minimum viable project to harden systems to protect against steal now, decrypt later risks.

Quantum Strategy Elements

The quantum business use cases (e.g., supply chain optimization) and gap analyses drive the quantum technology strategy. Best practices can be applied and tailored to implement (ITIL) and secure (NIST) quantum technologies. While best practices guide a quantum cybersecurity strategy, the quantum cybersecurity strategy is balanced and directed by the needs of the business (e.g., quantum business use cases). While numerous resources and templates are available about strategy contents, we advise organizations to develop their quantum technologies strategy based on the ITIL Strategy Management practice and project management best practice:

- **Purpose and vision:** Include the service owner's purpose and vision detailed in the quantum business case that supports the overall organizational vision,
- **Scope and authority:** Provide a list of what is in (Figure 3.3) and out of scope for the organization and details about the authorization to proceed with the quantum strategy, projects, and initiatives,

- **Organizational capabilities:** Describe and evaluate the organization's capabilities (people, process, and technology) to transition to, use, and optimize quantum technologies,
- **Gap analysis:** Summarize the analysis (e.g., internal and external, and people, process, and technology) and recommendations,
- **Objectives and key results:** List the main objectives and measurable results for the quantum technologies program of projects and initiatives,
- **Budget:** Develop a long-term and sustainable financial vision and budget for the quantum program (e.g., part of the organization's annual CapEx and OpEx budgeting process to determine future spending and investment priorities). The quantum budget is aligned with the organization's strategy, policies, and procedures,
- **Timelines:** Illustrate the timelines (e.g., Gantt chart, Figure 4.2 addressed later) and milestones for the quantum projects and initiatives,
- **Risks and issues:** Identify the most severe risks and impactful issues associated with the quantum program with risk and issue treatment plans. Organizations may adopt and tailor the *NIST IR 8286 Integrating Cybersecurity and Enterprise Risk Management* (2020) framework to guide risk management activities (including strategy governance),
- **Governance:** Align to the enterprise risk management strategy and outline roles, responsibilities, policies, processes, procedures, and general quantum program management, including monitoring, controlling, and reporting progress,
- **Project and initiatives:** Include the scope, rationale, objectives, budget, schedule, risks and issues, resources, deliverables, and other elements for each initiative and project. Include project objectives, for example:
  - *People*—provide supply chain and finance departments with Qiskit quantum software development training,

- *People*—hire a quantum software engineer, a quantum algorithm researcher, and a quantum business analyst (finance and supply chain process optimization),
- *People*—hire a quantum algorithm researcher (finance and supply chain) and a quantum business analyst (IT department),
- *Process*—implement Lean Six Sigma process optimization projects in the finance and supply chain departments,
- *Process*—initiate finance and supply chain algorithm research and optimize supply chain and finance workflows,
- *Technology*—procure QaaS from our cloud provider and set up a practice area to experiment with finance and supply chain quantum algorithms,
- *Technology*—upgrade and patch the organization's HPC environment to prepare for quantum technologies integration,
- *Technology*—implement quantum APIs between the organization's HPC environment and the QaaS platform,
- *Technology*—conduct an inventory of cryptographic assets managed and data handled by the organization, and create an inventory of the organization's suppliers of cryptographic assets, and so on.

- **Procurement:** Detail the procurement plan to support the quantum strategy including changes to support cryptographic agility,
- **Strategy conclusion:** The conclusion may outline the main points of the strategy and include recommendations and next steps. A goal of the strategy is to trigger and guide action. The conclusion has a *sales* element where the goal is to get approval. Therefore, storytelling and persuasion techniques are used.

Combine these technology strategy elements to support the business strategy and achieve the organization's vision and objectives by leveraging quantum technologies.

End of Service Strategy

Organizations are reminded that the "replacement of legacy [technologies] can be expensive and logistically complex" (Australian Signals Directorate 2024, 6). Therefore, organizations can benefit from an end-of-service strategy and technology disposal plan (also known as asset retirement) for displaced technologies to ensure a smooth ending to post-quantum cryptographic migrations and other technology projects involving legacy technologies. Legacy technologies are those meeting criteria like being at the end of their lifecycle, out of provider support, not cost-effective, difficult to update, and so on (Australian Signals Directorate 2024). The end-of-service life strategy and technology disposal plan can be aligned with the United Nations Sustainable Development Goals (SDG 12, Target 5) to reduce waste through prevention, reduction, recycling, and reuse. The organization can follow and tailor a project-oriented approach to asset disposal:

1. Identify the strategy, scope, and objectives for phasing out legacy technology (including responsible disposable practices, donating to communities in need, etc.).
2. Complete or access the inventory of legacy technology including software (e.g., legacy bill of materials that may be part of the organization's configuration management database). The inventory may be part of the quantum risk analysis where legacy cryptography is identified, and a quantum bill of materials report is produced.
3. Develop a technology phase-out-schedule and tactical plan (e.g., predisposition checklist) aligned with the introduction of quantum technologies (e.g., cutover strategy).
4. Deploy the new quantum technologies and phase-out legacy technologies.
5. Erase the data (permanently) from phased-out hardware, then recycle or donate for reuse.
6. Update service management records (e.g., configuration register).

The plan to implement quantum technologies, and update and replace post-quantum cryptography in an organization is strengthened with a technologies disposal plan and avoiding a *messy* end to migration projects where migration planners forgot to consider what to do with the old equipment! Therefore, in the plan and design phases, project planners elaborate a sustainable process to responsibly dispose of legacy equipment and permanently erase any associated data as per privacy best practices.

Thus, developing a technology strategy is a collaborative activity that benefits from iterations and socialization before it is approved by the organization's senior leadership. Creating a polished one-page quantum strategy infographic is a powerful resource when talking to people about quantum strategies. A quantum strategy infographic[*] is a resource that can be updated and reused for many years. As the business strategy drives the organization's technology strategy, the technology strategy drives the cybersecurity strategy. These three strategies are continual, concurrent, and consecutive: a journey rather than a set of dust-collecting documents.

Microlearning

Strategies form the foundation of a mature organization and IT department:

- Find strategy templates, guides, and other resources to develop a technology strategy that includes quantum technologies,
- Play strategy games and run simulations to improve your strategy competencies,
- Learn about sustainability in technology management best practices including disposition.

---

[*] Team building can be enhanced by inviting people to create the *official* quantum strategy infographic for the organization. Besides receiving powerful and informative infographics, one may also discover new creative talent on the team, who are engaged in the quantum vision and journey.

Quantum Cybersecurity Strategy

> **Quantum readiness:** The ability to manage risks related to quantum technologies in the categories of people, process, and technology including providing sufficient post-quantum cryptography, and developing and maintaining cryptographic agility. Quantum readiness assumes that a minimum viable cybersecurity foundation is maintained and continually optimized for both quantum and classical technologies.

The quantum cybersecurity strategy focuses on achieving quantum cybersecurity readiness by implementing post-quantum cryptography and achieving cryptographic agility, while the business quantum strategy is focused on leveraging the capabilities of quantum technologies. Increasingly, one finds more resources to guide the transition to post-quantum cryptography and achieving cryptographic agility; they uniformly recommend a phased and risk-based approach (i) plan, (ii) inventory and prioritize (risk identification and analysis), (iii) migrate and stabilize (risk treatment), and (iv) optimize (continual improvement). See the *References* section for a detailed list of authorities.

There are additional resources with similar procedures based on adaptive project delivery (e.g., iteratively plan, implement, and optimize). Another common recommendation in these documents is to start the journey to post-quantum cryptography and cryptographic agility as soon as possible.

The quantum cybersecurity strategy is a component of the technology strategy and builds upon the ITIL foundation of service management the organization has developed. Recall that ITIL service management is about managing digital technologies throughout their life cycle, including implementing new technologies like quantum computing, and phasing out legacy technologies that cannot be updated to accommodate post-quantum cryptography for example. Organizational leadership revisits its cybersecurity vision when updating the quantum technology and cybersecurity strategies.

Quantum Cybersecurity Vision

Earlier we wrote that vision statements guide the overall direction of the organization's unit, department, or service. The cybersecurity vision may include elements of preventing theft of sensitive information, ensuring received data is correct, and preventing unauthorized access to the organization's systems. For example, a cybersecurity vision statement might reflect the desire to be a leader in quantum-resistant cybersecurity to ensure the security of digital assets and to inspire confidence in partners, stakeholders, and customers. Following are two examples of a cybersecurity vision tuned for quantum technologies:

Vision Example 1: Leverage an adaptive digital foundation to develop, implement, maintain, and optimize a quantum-resistant ecosystem that safeguards our organization's systems and data from the disruptive potential of quantum and classical technologies.

Vision Example 2: We aim to provide quantum-safe technologies, establish layers of unwavering cyber defenses, and support a culture of cybersecurity readiness, to ensure data confidentiality, integrity, and availability.

The organization may also develop and include in the cybersecurity strategy supporting quantum cybersecurity goals such as:

- Align cybersecurity projects with the ITIL Service Management System to improve service quality and reduce risks,
- Provide diverse cryptographic protection for prioritized data and systems,
- Conduct a quantum risk analysis and develop a bill of materials,
- Develop an inventory of the organization's cryptographic assets, data handled, and supplier's cryptographic assets,
- Analyze vendor's and partner's quantum security strategies and plans and collaborate with like-minded organizations,
- Develop a post-quantum cryptography migration strategy and plan,
- Implement cryptographic agility optimization projects,

- And other goals specific to the unique organization on its path to quantum cybersecurity readiness.

High-level goals can be translated into objectives. Objectives are more specific and are measurable and objective. For example, quantum cybersecurity objectives may include:

- Procure the *QuantumPlus Cryptography Inventory v2.1* software by June next year,
- Complete Phase 3 of the *Essential Eight* cybersecurity foundation project by December next year,
- Hire a quantum application scientist and a quantum business analyst by the end of this year,
- Review and revise the business continuity plan and update for quantum cybersecurity risks by the end of June,
- Purchase the *What Now? Cybersecurity Simulation for Leadership* training program and arrange for a leadership cybersecurity competition during Cybersecurity Awareness Month next year,
- Select and test the NIST recommended algorithms (e.g., CRYSTALS–Dilithium) for the organization and update the security policies, procedures, and related documents by the end of this fiscal year,
- Develop a cryptographic agility procedure with checklists to quickly update or switch to another post-quantum cryptographic scheme by the end of the year.

The cybersecurity objectives can be implemented as projects and initiatives. Thus, IT and cybersecurity leadership develop and align the quantum cybersecurity vision, goals, and objectives to support the IT and business strategies. These are translated into security policies, procedures, projects, initiatives, training, templates, checklists, and processes.

Quantum Cybersecurity Risk Assessment

Developing the cybersecurity vision, goals, and objectives is necessary, but not sufficient; the organization is advised to understand the risks and issues that may interfere with achieving their strategies (e.g., the essence of enterprise risk management, NIST 2020b). Organizations are recommended to conduct a cybersecurity risk assessment (Figure 3.4) to determine the effectiveness and the upper limits of their data protection systems to prevent and mitigate a quantum-enabled cyberattack.[†] Indeed, quantum cybersecurity experts recommend conducting a risk assessment (also known as the *discovery* or inventory phase) early in their quantum journey. The risk assessment goal is to identify their most important assets and associated risks and prioritize treatment. If there is a security gap, sometimes a *simple* configuration change might be made to reach the desired level of cryptography or physical security might be improved; however, most organizations will likely require a series of post-quantum cryptographic migration projects to secure sensitive data and systems.

Next is a hypercritical and complex risk analysis that most organizations face, analyzing the level of migration urgency to post-quantum cryptography. The organization conducts a series of risk analyses to gain a holistic understanding of the current state of data and device cryptography and security. The assessors also determine how much effort (e.g., time and resources) is required to achieve the appropriate level of post-quantum cryptography through migration projects. The earlier the cryptographic inventory and assessment are completed (and thereafter maintained), the sooner the organization can confidently begin post-quantum cryptography projects. Waiting too long may result in hasty and costly migrations; indeed, the best consulting resources may already be hired on competitors' projects adding additional and compounding risks for late adopters! However, the first series of quantum cybersecurity

---

[†] The risk management approach in this book is based on ISO 31000 Risk Management and aligned with other standards like the PMBOK® Guide and frameworks like the NIST IR 8286 Integrating Cybersecurity and Enterprise Risk Management.

Identify Risks and Issues

- Cause **+** Risk or Issue Event **+** Effect

Analyse Risks and Issues

- Probability of Occurrence and Impact

Prioritize Treatment

- Prevent, Mitigate, Avoid, Accept, Transfer, etc.

Treatment Projects and Initiatives

- Cybersecurity Minimum Viable Foundation
- Quantum Awareness
- Project and Service Management Optimization
- Cryptographic Agility
- Quantum Technologies and Applications
- Post-Quantum Cryptographic Migrations

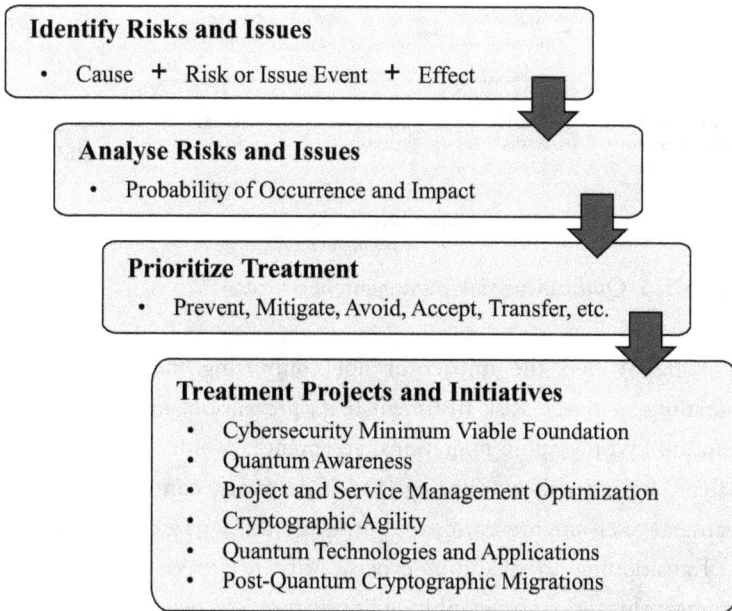

Figure 3.4 Quantum cybersecurity risk management process

projects can run concurrently to address any steal now, decrypt later risks.

In *Quantum Cybersecurity*, we provide a risk management approach[‡] that most organizations can generally apply (Figure 3.5). Organizations begin planning their quantum risk management approach by following generally accepted best practices[§] and developing quantum strategies: business, technology, and cybersecurity. Following risk planning, risk identification includes conducting a cryptographic inventory to identify devices and data susceptible to a quantum attack. Risk analysis guided by Mosca's Theorem (e.g., the probability quantum relevant technologies will appear before the organization migrates to post-quantum

---

[‡] We avoid repeating the fundamentals of risk management found in standards (e.g., ISO 31000 Risk Management) and frameworks (e.g., NIST enterprise risk management) that we combined in *Shields Up: Cybersecurity Project Management*.

[§] Recall that the value proposition in standards and frameworks is that with their judicial application and tailoring, there is a greater probability that risks may be reduced, and the planned level of quality may be achieved. Therefore, risk management begins with standards and frameworks.

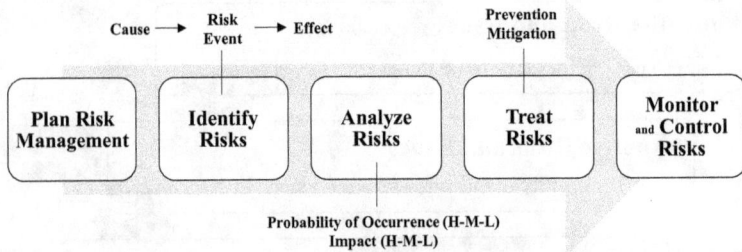

Figure 3.5 Qualitative risk management process

cryptography and the impact of not completing the cryptographic migrations in time). Risk treatment (e.g., prevention, mitigation, post-quantum cryptographic migrations, acceptance, avoidance) follows risk analysis. Project risk monitoring (and if necessary, controlling) follows treatment to ensure prevention and mitigation actions are successful.

Transitioning to quantum cybersecurity readiness—post-quantum cryptography and cryptographic agility (Figure 3.6) begin with business, technology, and cybersecurity strategies regarding people, process, and technology. At its core, cybersecurity is risk management. Our structured approach is based on ITIL's Service Value System, where strategy and demand drive quantum projects and initiatives to deliver value. Business, technology, and cybersecurity strategies are risk-based, evolve, and guide quantum technologies and applications adoption to support business quantum use cases (e.g., optimize customer service response and incident resolution). Technology projects are initiated to conduct cryptographic inventories, implement post-quantum cryptographic migration projects, and develop, maintain, and optimize cryptographic agility.

Simply, when one reads the literature from leading organizations like NIST (the United States), Agence Nationale de la Sécurité des Systèmes d'Information (ANSSI; France), Nationaal Bureau voor Verbindings-beveiliging (NBV; the Netherlands), European Telecommunications Standards Institute (ETSI; Europe), and others, the transition to post-quantum cybersecurity appears straightforward, albeit challenging, lengthy, and risky, and all recommend to begin the quantum journey without delay:

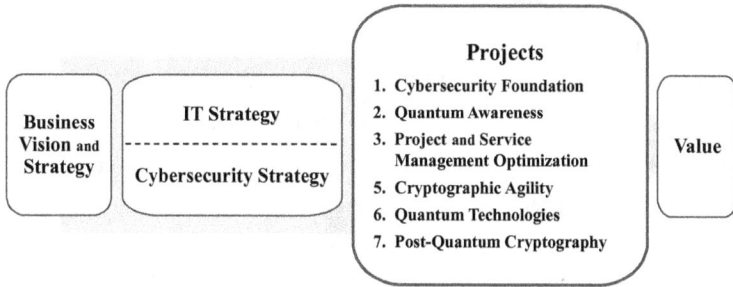

Business Vision and Strategy

IT Strategy

Cybersecurity Strategy

Projects
1. Cybersecurity Foundation
2. Quantum Awareness
3. Project and Service Management Optimization
5. Cryptographic Agility
6. Quantum Technologies
7. Post-Quantum Cryptography

Value

Figure 3.6 Pathway to quantum projects

1. Address any steal now, decrypt later risks with a minimum viable cybersecurity foundation,
2. Develop a quantum technology and cybersecurity strategy,
3. Conduct a cryptographic risk assessment (identify and analyze risks and issues),
4. Plan the post-quantum cryptographic migration (plan risk treatment),
5. Implement the post-quantum cryptographic migration project plan (e.g., referred to as a *roadmap* in some publications),
6. Implement and maintain cryptographic agility through projects and continual improvement initiatives.

This straightforward project approach aligns with best practices widely found in standards and frameworks. It is best practice to include those closest to the risks such as the technology and security architects, business leaders, vendors, and others; indeed, the technical leadership will lead the quantum risk analyses and formulate risk treatment plans. Before proceeding with a comprehensive risk identification and analysis, the reader may review best practices found in ISO 31000 Risk Management or NIST IR 8286 Integrating Cybersecurity and Enterprise Risk Management to assure a high-quality risk assessment.

Quantum Risk Identification

Risk identification follows risk planning for quantum technologies including cybersecurity. The NIST Cybersecurity Framework and other frameworks (e.g., ITIL) include best practices to identify and analyze risks for the technology ecosystem's *current state*. Then develop treatment plans to achieve the desired *future state* (also known as the *target* state) for major strategic projects. In the NIST Cybersecurity Framework, the *identify* function aligns with quantum risk identification and the cryptographic discovery inventory. The quantum cybersecurity future state includes migrating to post-quantum cryptography and achieving cybersecurity readiness (Figure 2.5). The risk assessment is focused on achieving the target state and determining the degree of urgency.

The NIST (2022b) Integrating Cybersecurity and Enterprise Risk Management framework, ISO 31000 Risk Management, and the PMBOK® Guide all provide a common approach and the foundation for risk management used in *Quantum Cybersecurity* (Figure 3.5). There are two risk identification techniques: general and focused. General risk identification broadly considers risks such as those related to cryptographic agility. The project manager facilitates the discussion to identify, analyze, and treat risks as they are mentioned.

The focused risk identification technique narrows the questions about a single topic, such as what are the cryptographic agility risks related to people? What are the cryptographic agility risks for our preferred suppliers? Therefore, the team can analyze category by category of risks like cryptographic agility risks. While there are many ways to categorize risks, we offer three broad categories for a quick start: (i) current cybersecurity risk posture regarding a minimum viable cybersecurity foundation, (ii) post-quantum cryptography, and (iii) cryptographic agility (Figure 3.7).

There are no doubt other ways to guide a focused risk assessment and we invite the reader to tailor their own. Organizations are advised to take a methodical and comprehensive approach to risk assessment due to the multidimensionality and severity of quantum risks and issues.

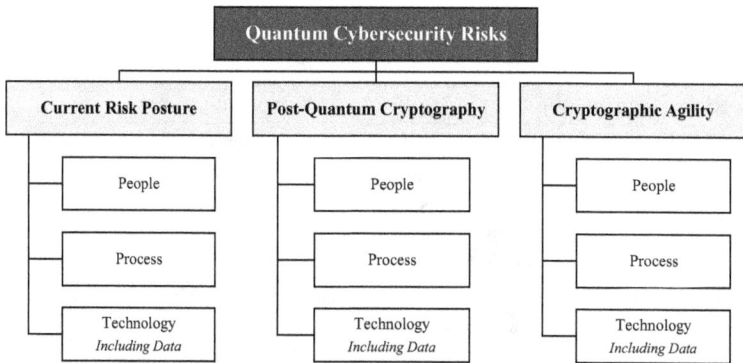

Figure 3.7 *Focused quantum cybersecurity risk assessment*

Risk identification includes the risk cause, the risk event, and the risk effect on the project or initiative if the risk is realized (Table 3.4 and Figure 3.5). The risk assessment includes the (i) degree of urgency to act (prevent and mitigate quantum cybersecurity risks and resolve issues) and the (ii) severity of quantum cybersecurity risks facing the organization. Severity reflects the probability the risk may occur, and its impact (*Probability* X *Impact* = *Risk Severity*). Prioritize any high-severity risks and high-impact issues immediate attention.

The quantum risk assessment helps identify severe risks and is a critical step toward quantum readiness.

Since each organization is unique with complex systems, quantifying risks (e.g., quantitative risk analysis with the Monte Carlo Simulation) related to quantum cybersecurity threats is challenging, effort-intensive, and perhaps not the best use of time. Instead, organizations can complete more expedient analyses with a qualitative risk analysis (high, medium, or low). Organizations may go beyond the broad categories seen in Figure 3.7 and identify risks related to the attack surface, infrastructure, data, partner dependency, target probability, system analysis, migration urgency, cryptographic agility, and commercial effects:

Attack surface: Identify quantum cybersecurity risks with the IT and security architects related to the organization's infrastructure. Then, analyze their impact (e.g., high, medium, or low) upon the

Table 3.4 Classical risk assessment example

Risk Element	Description
Risk identification	Risk statement: due to the progress toward a cryptographically-relevant quantum computer (cause), there is a risk the organization's assets may be attacked (risk), resulting in data breaches, intellectual property theft, financial damage, and so on (effect)
Risk analysis	Probability of occurrence: analyze the likelihood of the risk occurring (high, medium, or low)
	Impact to project or organization: analyze the impact to the organization or project if the risk occurs (high, medium, or low)
	Calculate[a] the *Risk Severity = Probability × Impact*
Risk treatment	Identify prevention actions, like protecting the organization against steal now and decrypt later, and mitigation actions, like regularly updating detect, respond, and recover capabilities. Other common treatment options include risk transfer, avoidance, and acceptance

[a]To calculate risk severity (probability of occurrence X impact), the qualitative measures are assigned quantitative values: high = 3, medium = 2, and low = 1. Therefore, a high probability risk with medium impact would be $3 \times 2 = 6/9$ severity. This simple calculation is useful in risk registers to sort risks by severity and prioritized for monitoring and control (if necessary).

organization and probability of occurrence (e.g., high, medium, or low). For this risk and others, a qualitative risk management can quickly determine the risk severity.

Infrastructure: Identify the types of systems, capabilities (including processes and people), and infrastructure the organization uses then analyze the risk if the systems are attacked with a cryptographically-relevant quantum computer. Both attack surface and infrastructure risk assessments and recommendations for prevention and mitigation (e.g., the *Essential Eight*) are increasingly available online for further study. Organizations are advised to prioritize the treatment for any steal now, decrypt later risks (e.g., establish a minimum viable cybersecurity foundation).

Data: Identify and analyze the types of data and information the organization uses in terms of criticality, disclosure sensitivity, and effect of unauthorized and undetected modifications. Mosca's

QUANTUM TRANSITION STRATEGIES   89

Theorem, presented later, provides guidance to analyze risks related to data.

Partner dependency: Identify and analyze the dependencies on external partners, vendors, customers, and so on.

Target probability: Determine probability the organization might be attacked with quantum technologies; for example, organizations that provide healthcare services likely have a higher target probability than an atelier in Fairlight, Saskatchewan, that crafts prized leather wallets, purses, and accessories.

System analysis: Identify and analyze risks related to the organization's technology, information management, and industrial control systems and the contents they protect (e.g., key stores, root keys, signing keys, sensitive personally identifiable information [PII], passwords). Determine which systems interact and the type of data shared (internal and external).

Migration urgency: Determine how quickly the organization needs to migrate to post-quantum cryptography. Analyze the impact (high, medium, or low) for this risk category. Regulator pressures may accelerate migration urgency. Mosca's Theorem and the Crypto Agility Risk Assessment Framework can be used to analyze data migration urgency (personal and organizational). Assessing migration urgency is a crucial and prioritized activity.

Cryptographic agility: Related to post-quantum cryptographic risks are cryptographic agility risks; organizations value the ability to quickly update their cryptography to remain safe and secure (e.g., only *update* algorithms rather than *replace* endpont technologies).

Commercial effects: There are nontechnical risks related to a post-quantum cryptographic attack to analyze including financial loss and reputation damage. There may also be compliance effects such as business restrictions, fines, and other penalties. Finally, there could be impaired growth due to a post-quantum cryptographic attack. Analyzing commercial risks may be improved if an organization's legal and risk specialists participate (e.g., they can contribute to better understanding risks like providing ethical advice about treating quantum risks or implications of multiple international jurisdictions and regulatory schemes).

As risk management is continuous, these categories may be monitored to identify new risks and issues. Thus, the project manager, IT, and security architects can use well-regarded risk assessment techniques like those detailed in the NIST IR 8286 Integrating Cybersecurity and Enterprise Risk Management, ISO/IEC 31010:2019—Risk Management—Risk Assessment Techniques, the PMBOK® Guide, and Mosca's Theorem to manage quantum risks and issues (Figures 3.4 and 3.5). For example, the risk and issue register are generally accepted to regularly manage risks and issues including cybersecurity.

However, it is unclear when a quantum computer can break classical encryption methods. Sometimes emerging technologies follow an uneven development trajectory, resulting in a risk that a quantum computer with sufficient hacking capabilities may arrive sooner than expected. Quantum researchers monitor research and development trends to predict the arrival of quantum technologies. Dr. Michele Mosca is one such researcher monitoring quantum timelines and developed a theorem to guide a focused risk analysis related to post-quantum cryptographic migration urgency (Mosca and Piani, 2023).

Mosca's Theorem

Michelle Mosca and his research team have developed a quantum timeline risk analysis approach represented mathematically:

$$\text{Mosca's Theorem } (X + Y) > Z$$

According to Mosca's Theorem $(X + Y) > Z$, when the amount of time that data must remain secure (X) plus the project time it takes to achieve sufficient post-quantum cryptographic protection (Y) is greater than when cryptographically-relevant quantum computers become available and powerful enough to break classical cryptography (Z), the organization has run out of time and their systems, and data are

Scenario **1**: **PQC Migration is Late**

| **X** Data Security Duration | **Y** Transition Time to PQC |

| **Z** Time to a CRQC |

Secret Keys Compromised   ☹

Increasing risk of steal now, decrypt later   Time

Scenario **2**: **PQC Migration Completed In Time**

| **X** Data Security Duration | **Y** Transition Time to PQC | ☺

| **Z** Time to a CRQC |

Increasing risk of steal now, decrypt later   Time

Legend Mosca's Theorem Scenario 1: $(X+Y) > Z$ = Trouble!

Mosca's Theorem Scenario 2: $Z > (X+Y)$ = Project Success!

PQC: Post-quantum cryptography

CRQC: Cryptographically-relevant quantum computer

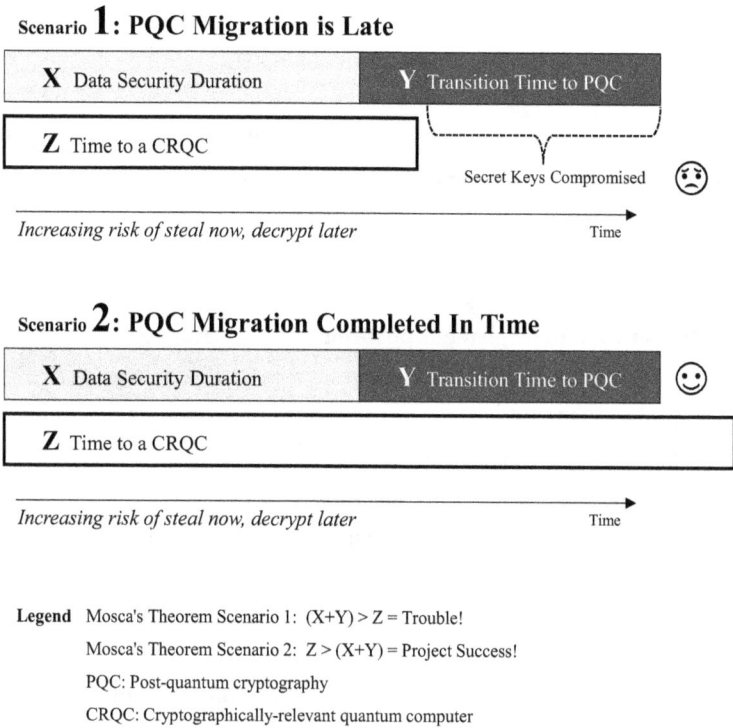

Figure 3.8 Quantum threat timelines in Mosca's Theorem

at risk.¶ Organizations apply Mosca's Theorem to analyze and treat risks
(Figure 3.8, after Palo Alto Networks Inc. 2023, 15).

A goal of this book is to assist readers to reduce the project time
it takes to achieve sufficient post-quantum cryptographic protection
(Mosca's Y parameter).

Data security duration (X): Organizations begin their quantum
risk analysis by understanding how long encryption is needed
to secure their data sets. Organizations have multiple data sets
like personally identifiable information and corporate intellectual
property, with varying degrees of sensitivity and criticality. Some
data must be kept secure for only a few years, like credit card

---

¶ Readers may pause, re-read this paragraph, and reflect upon this critical and
indispensable risk analysis technique that guides the quantum program of
projects.

information that is relevant until the card's expiration date, then
the value of the data declines. Medical data and other data might
be relevant for decades as directed by regulatory bodies, requiring
more extended periods of protection for up to 50 years (Canadian
Forum for Digital Infrastructure Resilience 2023, 5). Organizations can prioritize their data sets (e.g., data classified as *high
value*) during the project plan and design phases for subsequent
post-quantum cryptographic migrations.

Project time to implement post-quantum cryptography (Y): The
project team is tasked to answer the most dreaded question in
project management: "How long will it take?" And in a quantum
cybersecurity risk analysis, the organization estimates the time to
migrate a set of quantum-safe tools (e.g., post-quantum cryptographic algorithms to protect and secure prioritized data and
systems). Estimating activity durations is the purview of project
time management and we have detailed that process and tools in
Shields Up (Skulmoski 2022).

Time to a cryptographically-relevant quantum computer (Z):
The third parameter in Mosca's Theorem represents the time
until a cryptographically-relevant quantum computer arrives that
can break public-key encryption. Indeed, there is a degree
of uncertainty to when a cryptographically-relevant quantum
computer may arrive. This third parameter is external to
organizations and out of their control. However, IT and security
architects monitor technological milestones like qubit development progress, error correction advances, and when a quantum
computer may break a 2048-bit Rivest–Shamir–Adleman (RSA)
key** to analyze the time to a cryptographically-relevant quantum
computer. Mosca and Piani (2023) monitor the quantum threat
timelines and produce publicly available progress reports to help

---

** It would take around 300 trillion years for a classical computer to break a
RSA-2048 bit encryption key when one searches online for estimates. We are
less interested in a precise number (200 to 300 trillion or even billion years is
still a lot to hack into a computer), and instead, we are more interested in the
order of magnitude required to break classical public encryption when
quantum supremacy is achieved.

quantum champions predict the arrival of a cryptographically-relevant quantum computer.

Therefore, the organization analyzes the degree their data sets are vulnerable to a quantum-relevant attack and the urgency to protect the data (personal and organizational); in essence, "how long does the data need to be protected?" Mosca guides us to conduct an internal risk assessment (data security duration and project transition timelines to post-quantum cryptography) and external risk assessments (arrival time of a cryptographically-relevant quantum computer). The technical leadership team will analyze data, estimate the duration to migrate to post-quantum cryptography projects, and predict when a cryptographically-relevant quantum computer may arrive (Figure 3.8). Some might factor in additional time for post-quantum cryptographic migrations if their organization is not likely an immediate target and not in a critical infrastructure industry like defense or healthcare. Therefore, a key cybersecurity goal is to reduce the transition time to post-quantum cryptography (Y); that is, organizations desire a lean project-oriented approach to minimize the time to cybersecurity readiness (post-quantum cryptography and cryptographic agility) should a cryptographically-relevant quantum computer arrive earlier than predicted.

Organizations will not be able to protect their systems and data from quantum attacks ($X + Y > Z$) if the quantum threat timeline for cryptographically-relevant quantum computers (Z) is shorter than the data security requirements (X) and transition project durations (Y). A risk statement may be written to fully describe the risk (Figure 3.8, Scenario 1):

> *Risk cause*: due to the growing investments and government grants in quantum technologies,
> *Risk event*: there is a risk a cryptographically-relevant quantum computer may arrive sooner than anticipated,
> *Risk effect*: resulting in two potential high-impact effects: (i) the organization's data and systems are exposed to quantum risks sooner than expected and (ii) the available project time is

reduced to implement minimum viable cybersecurity, post-quantum cryptographic migrations, and digital agility projects.

Thus, a severe risk is a cryptographically-relevant quantum computer emerges before an organization completes its post-quantum cryptography migrations (the *Mosca Inequality*). Should an organization discover they do not have enough time to transition to post-quantum cryptographic solutions, and the time to a cryptographically-relevant quantum computer is imminent, the quantum cybersecurity team can prioritize systems and data to protect so if the organization is the target of a quantum attack, perhaps only less sensitive and critical data might be exfiltrated or compromised. The organization can add extra resources and crash and fast track prioritized projects; however, these techniques can be expensive and risky.

We can learn from previous cryptographic migrations (e.g., replacing SHA-1[††] with SHA-2 hash functions) that required long project timelines as we analyze risks with Mosca's Theorem. Applying Mosca's Theorem $(X + Y) > Z$ indicates a late post-quantum cryptographic migration program (Scenario 1, Figure 3.8), leaving the organization exposed to risks (e.g., the classical public cryptographic keys can be broken). Indeed, some suggest that $(X + Y)$ may "easily exceed two decades" (Cloud Security Alliance 2019, 7). Thus, quantum champions monitor *Q-Day*, the arrival of a cryptographically-relevant quantum computer.

Quantum champions, organizational and executive support, and lean project management can prevent and mitigate many quantum risks with a systematic approach based on best practices to complete post-quantum cryptographic migrations before a cryptographically-relevant quantum computer emerges (Scenario 2, Figure 3.8). A decade of

---

[††] The SHA-1 algorithm had design flaws that were only discovered after it was widely adopted and used. The initial post-quantum cryptographic algorithms might also have similar flaws discovered only after widespread adoption necessitating quick upgrades (e.g., cryptographic agility) to more secure cryptography and the recommendation for cryptographic agility. See Perryman et al. (2024) for more about previous cryptographic migrations (e.g., cryptographic migration project lessons learned).

projects can be implemented successfully with a lean project and service management approach aligned with risk and quality management best practices found in standards and frameworks (Table 2.1).

Therefore, there is a strong and convincing case to prepare for the quantum era of opportunities and threats. Indeed, waiting introduces the risk that when the organization desires post-quantum cryptographic migration consulting assistance, there may be a shortage of expertise should early adopters have the best subject matter experts already engaged. There is another severe risk that due to the desire to gain a strategic advantage, some research and development might not be made public, resulting in a cryptographically-relevant quantum computer emerging sooner than anticipated (Scenario 1, Figure 3.8). We aim to help organizations protect their most sensitive systems and data with post-quantum cryptography ahead of threat actors accessing a cryptographically-relevant computer. While the Mosca Theorem is a popular approach to analyze the organization's quantum risks, the Crypto Agility Risk Management Framework (CARAF) offers another approach should the organization need additional decision-making data.

Crypto Agility Risk Management Framework

For organizations wishing to include costs in their risk assessments, the CARAF is an alternative approach (FS-ISAC 2023a). The purpose of the CARAF risk assessment approach is to analyze, evaluate, and quantify the risk (financial costs) due to insufficient cryptographic agility (e.g., post-quantum cryptographic algorithms have not been implemented).

The CARAF risk assessment is an extension of the Mosca risk assessment to determine the cost of updating each asset to a secure state within the required timeframe. That is, one determines the duration their data needs to be secure (X parameter), the transition time to post-quantum cryptography (Y parameter), and the time a cryptographically-relevant quantum computer emerges (Z parameter). Then, one calculates the cost to migrate the prioritized assets to post-quantum cryptography. The organization has a quantitative measure to undertake a cost/benefit analysis to identify those assets where the asset value is greater than the cost to migrate to quantum-safe solutions (e.g., determine the minimum viable post-quantum cryptographic migration).

Think about: "Then, one calculates the cost to migrate the prioritized assets to post-quantum cryptography." Yes, this is no doubt a complex and time-consuming task to analyze and evaluate the costs associated with a multifaceted (people, process, and technology) program of projects, spanning perhaps a decade or more. It may be less important to complete a comprehensive cost/benefit analysis if the organization is mandated through regulation to transition to post-quantum cryptography. However, should the reader desire a detailed explanation of the CARAF risk assessment, and implementation guidance, the authors have published their approach (Chujuao et al. 2021). While the CARAF risk assessment provides additional information, most organizations are likely to first apply the Mosca's risk assessment and if they need additional information for certain data sets, the organization may apply the CARAF technique.

A Closer Look at Data

What data should be analyzed for risk and prioritized for treatment in Mosca's or the CARAF risk assessment? Two common types of data that may be long-lasting and targets for quantum cyberattackers are (i) personally identifiable information and (ii) sensitive organizational data. Personally identifiable information (PII) has a long life span, is a regular cyberattack target, and will continue to attract cyber threats (Table 3.5).

Organizations may also have sensitive data that are classified for most external parties and require long-term protection (Table 3.6). Sensitive organizational data are different from personal data in that personal data needs to be kept secret to protect the privacy of people, whereas organizational data need to be protected to safeguard the organization. Both types of data are at risk of steal now, decrypt later attacks.

In CISA's (2022) *Preparing Critical Infrastructure for Post-Quantum Cryptography*, they highlight the urgency to plan and implement post-quantum cryptography projects and identified national critical functions for prioritization. Some national critical functions

Table 3.5 Personally identifiable information

Full name	Social security number	Date of birth
Home address	Email address	Phone number
Driver's license number	Passport number	Banking information
Military identification	Photographs	And so on

Table 3.6 Organizational sensitive data

Organizational Data		
Customer information	Bank account information	Loan information
Income statements	Financial statements	Transaction details
Financial forecasts	Credit card statements	Payment card information
Employee information	Tax information	Wire transfer details
Asset valuation details	Formulas and recipes	Manufacturing procedures
Business strategy	Research and development	Computer source code
Pricing details	Technical data	Marketing strategy
Contracts and agreements	Intellectual property	State secrets
Minutes	Emails	And so on

are especially vulnerable due to data with long-term confidentiality requirements (CISA 2019, 3):

- Provide internet-based content, information, and communication services,
- Protect sensitive information,
- Provide satellite access network services,
- Support community health,
- Provide wireless access network services,
- Provide information technology products and services,
- Enforce law and provide defense,
- Maintain access to medical records.

While the list is American, it is useful guidance for organizations providing these functions to immediately start the post-quantum cryptography journey and can use Mosca's Theorem (Figure 3.8)

Table 3.7 Data classification

Military Classification	Classification by Value	Classification by Access
Top secret	High value	Restricted
Secret	Medium value	Confidential
Confidential	Low value	Internal
Public	—	Public

to determine the duration required to keep their data secure. Therefore, organizations can analyze their cryptography risks by examining personal and sensitive organizational data, and determining the risk probability (high, medium, or low) and impact (high, medium, or low) if the risk occurs. Some classify their data (Table 3.7) to standardize their risk management approach where any data classified as *high value* is prioritized for treatment (e.g., protect against steal now and migrate to post-quantum cryptography).

ITIL's service management catalog and the configuration management register can be updated with data classification details with the risk analysis results. The analysis is likely to include external stakeholder's data requiring additional risk analysis time and effort. Indeed, data can change over time such as a credit card number that eventually expires and its value diminishes. Conducting a data risk assessment is complex; however, a methodical approach can provide a framework to progress and gain an understanding of the organization's data in use, in transit, and at rest.

Microlearning.   Risk management, including quantum risk assessment, is a critical success factor for organizations, IT departments, and cybersecurity programs. Assessing quantum cybersecurity risks generally, and the risks-related data, guides the organization's post-quantum cryptography migration program. Readers can find additional guidance online:

- Find resources about post-quantum migration and risk assessments like the risk matrix, risk assessment frames of reference, and so on,
- Review other materials related to Mosca's Theorem,
- Learn about breaking the 2048-bit RSA cryptography; it's a critical milestone!

Vendor and Partner Assessment

Most organizations and their systems operate as part of an ecosystem interconnected with the partners', vendors', regulators', and customers' systems. Therefore, the quantum cybersecurity threat landscape is likely larger than threats to only the organization's internal digital ecosystem; external stakeholders' risks may be pushed to the organization. Therefore, organizations should assess their external stakeholders for post-quantum cryptographic readiness and agility. For example, have partners completed a cryptographic inventory? Do they have a transition plan to post-quantum cryptography? Is their solution a hybrid cryptographic environment? And so forth (FS-ISA 2023, 23). Analyzing vendors' and partners' risks is problematic at best since self-reported evaluations are susceptible to overly optimistic reports involving validity and reliability issues (e.g., confirmation bias). There is an increasing number of questionnaires (vendor attestation documents) found online to evaluate the post-quantum cryptographic posture and roadmap of an organization's partners, vendors, and other stakeholders. The post-quantum cryptographic inventories from external stakeholders can be evaluated to determine the degree of alignment with the organization's security policies and procedures (e.g., begin with the analysis in Table 3.3).

Quantum Relevant Milestones

Those interested in quantum technologies and their dual potentialities monitor milestones and use Mosca's Theorem to evaluate the state of quantum computing as it pertains to their organization. Quantum champions monitor milestones related to quantum computing research and development progress, regulations, hardware, applications, and cryptography including:

- Post-quantum cryptography algorithms: Monitor the quantum-safe algorithms endorsed by NIST throughout the standardization and stabilization process.
- Cryptographically-relevant quantum computer: Monitor the arrival of a quantum computer with sufficient capabilities to break public-key systems (e.g., asymmetric cryptography).
- Quantum machine learning applications: Monitor vendors' quantum strategies to add quantum capabilities to finance, healthcare, manufacturing, supply chain, and other business applications (e.g., supply chain management software with AI capabilities powered by quantum technologies).
- Personal device cryptography: Apple's PQ3 post-quantum cryptographic protocol for end-to-end secure messaging with advanced hybrid cryptography (e.g., Elliptic Curve Diffie–Hellman and CRYSTALS–Kyber encapsulation) signals mainstream acceptance for post-quantum cryptography.
- Quantum internet development: Progress to update the internet for quantum repeaters and nodes for quantum key distribution (QKD).

There are likely other milestones the reader will monitor (e.g., industry-specific quantum devices like quantum sensors for weather and environmental event forecasting).

The point is organizations monitor *external* developments to evaluate quantum-related risks as part of their risk analysis. The most critical *internal* quantum risk evaluation exercise is to conduct a cryptographic inventory.

Cryptographic Inventory

> *Most organizations have no clear view of the cryptographic technologies used by their existing Information Management (IM), Information Technology (IT) and Operational Technology (OT) systems; this will make it difficult to discover and then prioritize the systems to be upgraded to post-quantum cryptography* (Canadian Forum for Digital Infrastructure Resilience 2023, 4).

A critical step in assessing quantum risks is to conduct a cryptographic inventory (also known as *discovery*). Organizations can undertake two related inventories: (i) cryptography and (ii) data. The purpose of the cryptographic inventory is to discover, create, and maintain the network of hardware and middleware (including *every* IoT device, sensor, embedded device, smartwatch, pacemaker, and other end-point devices), APIs, and software (including public key infrastructure, file systems, virtualization, Software as a Service, blockchain, and more) that handle and manage encrypted communications. The inventory will help to analyze what is and what is not quantum-ready. The end-to-end pathways of data—internal and external—need to be documented and analyzed (e.g., data in use, at rest, and in transit).

There are at least four goals of the cryptographic inventory process (FS-ISAC 2023b inventory) and they can be adopted and tailored by an organization's cybersecurity experts:

1. Determine the *W5 + H (journalistic questions)* of who, what, when, where, why, and how data are created and used,
2. Document what is within the organization's control and should be monitored, controlled, and tracked through to digital readiness,
3. Identify what is external to the organization and its post-quantum cryptography status including hybrid cryptography,
4. Make the cryptographic inventory comprehensive (people, process, and technology).

These goals may be included in the inventory project charter and plan to orient the team. The cryptographic infrastructure is broad as it includes internal and external stakeholder's digital ecosystems, including any industrial systems (e.g., Supervisory Control and Data Acquisition [SCADA] systems and industrial control IoT devices like environmental sensors). Therefore, since the inventory is both internal and external, representing people, processes, and technologies, there will likely be multiple cryptographic inventories to create, collate, analyze, and maintain. The IT and security architects will use the inventory to analyze cryptographic risk: identify and analyze quantum susceptible (e.g., RSA) and resistant (e.g., CRYSTALS–Kyber) cryptography.

Since cybersecurity is broader than technologies (e.g., encryption keys and algorithms), the inventory should identify the business processes that use cryptography, and the people who use and *own* the systems and data from a service management perspective. The organization develops an inventory of cryptographic interdependencies within and among systems to understand the risks a post-quantum cryptographically-relevant attack poses to the organization. Yes, completing, maintaining, and optimizing the inventory is a significant undertaking that calls out for lean service and project management formality to improve the probability of long-term inventory success.

The cryptographic inventory (e.g., products, algorithms, and protocols) is a fundamental input to completing a risk analysis of the organization's exposure to a quantum cyberattack. The cryptographic inventory is also a critical success factor for cryptographic agility and for the respond and recover functions in a cybersecurity incident (e.g., disaster recovery and resiliency). A key point is the inventory is developed and *maintained* (and later optimized); as cryptographic and agility projects and initiatives progress, the inventory is updated to reflect the evolving cryptographic ecosystem. However, there are many risks related to the large number of systems and devices often widely deployed that need to be analyzed during and after the inventory project; indeed, some vendors may no longer be in business and unable to update their cryptography. The organization may consider designing a comprehensive inventory structure (beginning with details in Tables 3.8 and 3.9) and maintaining it as part of its cryptographic agility program.

From these two tables, one quickly appreciates the broad scope and complexity of a cryptographic inventory project that necessitates formal project management delivery approaches and techniques (Figure 2.8): "Performing a data protection inventory is usually one of the most time-consuming and difficult phases of the project and it helps to break it down into smaller subtasks" (Cloud Security Alliance 2021, 21). Indeed, multiple discovery tools and reports may need to be consolidated into the organization's cryptographic inventory and service management catalog. In our Design Workshop section, we recommend the team map out end-to-end processes and tools[‡‡] beginning with a comprehensive and perhaps series of inventories, to risk analysis and treatment, through to post-quantum cryptographic migration records management. The inventory analysis is an input into the organization's enterprise risk management process.

The second inventory is about the type and location of data in the organization. Again, inventory tools can automate the process and the tools can be customized to categorize data in meaningful ways to the organization (e.g., Tables 3.8 and 3.9, after the Cloud Security Alliance 2021, 21). The inventory team will manually validate the accuracy of key data sets.

These activities (and others to account for the full technical stack) can be estimated and added to the cryptographic inventory schedule. For reporting purposes, a cryptographic inventory table may be developed (Table 3.9).

Organizations may tailor and go beyond the details in Tables 3.8 and 3.9. The inventory will likely be complex as technology can have layers of security that require discovery and documentation. For example, many computer components like the firmware and software applications have built-in cryptography. Some of this cryptography is hard coded and cannot be changed by the user, while others can be

---

[‡‡] We use the *Yellow Stickie* method to design our projects where stickie note pads are distributed to the team in design workshops, and the team members design the end-to-end project or migration in this case. Provide different color stickie note pads and markers to enhance creativity.

Table 3.8 Cryptographic inventory fields example

Component	Considerations
Hardware	• List the available ciphers (hardware-based encryption) and updatable firmware
Applications	• Identify in-house and vendor applications and their cryptography • Identify critical and high-availability applications including blockchain technologies leveraging public key cryptography • Inventory internal and external application connections including Software as a Service in the cloud • Identify the processes and details for applications using cryptography
Endpoints	• Understand where the data are stored and secured (e.g., server details) • Identify the devices used to access data and how they are protected
Network	• Document how data flow into, through, and out of the organization's network and the devices that protect the data in transit • Identify any high-risk components
Cloud providers	• Get information about cloud provider's roadmaps[a] that support post-quantum cryptography including APIs • Identify keys, configurations, and ciphers
Third party	• Get information about vendor strategies and project plans to support post-quantum cryptography and cryptographic agility • Add post-quantum cryptography requirements to procurement practices and clauses (e.g., request for proposal documents)
Data	• Identify and categorize the organization's sensitive and critical datasets and its users • Identify the duration the organization's data assets require protection (see also Tables 3.8 and 3.9) • Document how the data are secured by applications • Determine the risk severity from a steal now, decrypt later attack
Regulatory	• Identify, categorize, and prioritize any data sets (Table 3.10) under regulatory control

(Continued)

Table 3.8 (Continued)

Component	Considerations
Blind spots	• List any device or application using cryptographic methods not visible or not configurable by an administrator. Blind spots require monitoring, and an issue might be raised and added to the risk and issue register

aRoadmap is a common term used in post-quantum cryptographic documents which refers to the project plan. Unfortunately, the reader is required to decipher these *code words* to understand exactly their meaning. Therefore, we align with standards and frameworks and apply their terminology to reduce the risk of misunderstanding (e.g., roadmaps and challenges versus project plans and risks).

Table 3.9 Cryptographic inventory reporting example

Element	Description
System	Identify the system (internal or external), service owner, and other relevant details with a link to the service catalog
Algorithm	Identify the algorithm class (e.g., AES-256, RSA, Elliptic Curve Digital Signature Algorithm [ECDSA], Elliptic Curve Diffie–Hellman [ECDH; Elliptic Curve Encryption], DAS [Finite Field Encryption], etc.)
Type	List the type of cryptography (e.g., symmetric, asymmetric, hash, etc.)
Purpose	Identify the cryptography's use (e.g., encryption/confidentiality, integrity, signatures, key establishment, etc.)
Criticality	Evaluate the value or criticality of the asset to the organization
Treatment	Determine the treatment (e.g., larger key sizes required, no longer secure, asset to be disposed of, etc.)
Risk status	Evaluate the risk (or issue) status: red—out of control and likely to become an issue, amber —in control but might become an issue, green—in control and unlikely to become an issue

upgraded. Some vendors might not have plans to provide post-quantum cryptography updates. Some applications might be custom software where the cryptography updates may need to be managed as new requirements. For these issues, document the details in the risk and issue register and develop and implement issue resolution plans (e.g., a program of quantum cybersecurity projects and initiatives). The inventory teams will manually validate key inventory results to reduce inaccuracy risks.

Again, the inventory can be planned as a project with collaborative workshops. The project manager brings the project management discipline to the inventory planning process (e.g., inventory scope, schedule, budget, and a RACI chart to identify inventory roles and responsibilities) and the cybersecurity team brings the technical content and leads technical planning. We advocate the inventory process be planned through to technology disposition with the understanding that the inventory process is an ongoing activity and part of the organization's technology management and governance practices (e.g., ITIL).

The cybersecurity team can find online resources to manage the technical aspects of the inventory like flowcharts (Canadian Forum for Digital Infrastructure Resilience 2023, 15) and recommended inventory fields like the location of sensitive data and devices, criticality, and sensitivity of data to the organization, algorithm type, maximum configurable key size, and so on (Cloud Security Alliance 2021, 21). These requirements should be considered when procuring, configuring, and using cryptographic inventory and discovery tools. The inventory range and complexity may be seen in Tables 3.8 and 3.9 (after Palo Alto Networks Inc. 2023, 19–21) and will guide inventory planning, including scope, duration estimating, sequencing, scheduling, and risk management (e.g., risk identification, analysis, and treatment). The inventory scope will be comprehensive and may include information technology, information management, and industrial control systems.

Discovery Tools

While it is possible to conduct a manual inventory of the organization's cryptography, using automated tools is the preferred method to gain a deep understanding of the cryptography protecting sensitive data (in use, at rest, and in transit) and devices. Automated inventory tools are more amenable to manual inventory collection and management. Given the complexity of organizations (e.g., a mix of information technologies, information management, and industrial control systems) the organization may require multiple tools to cover different technologies or to provide specific information. The goal is to identify, document, and analyze all data sources and devices using cryptography in the technological ecosystem (internal and external) followed by prioritization and risk treatment projects and initiatives. The project team estimates the time and resources required to complete the inventory. By understanding the inventory scope (e.g., Tables 3.8 and 3.9), the team can create realistic project and initiative plans. The ITIL Service Management Framework can be used to capture cryptographic inventory details (e.g., configuration management and part of a minimum viable foundation to manage quantum technologies).

A future benefit of documenting and maintaining the cryptographic and infrastructure inventories (e.g., ITIL configuration and service catalog management practices) is for severe cybersecurity breaches. In the case of a severe cybersecurity incident, the organization may invite an external response team to provide supplemental and specialized services. During incident investigations, external incident response teams will routinely request details about the organization's cryptographic inventory. The infrastructure and cryptography documentation will help the external incident response team to quickly respond and recover. Working with incomplete or outdated information can lead to detrimental incident response effects like alerting the attacker or accidentally destroying evidence.

Therefore, the IT and security architects will design the post-quantum cryptographic inventory not only for migration purposes but also to provide critical infrastructure and cryptographic details for routine service management, cybersecurity incident management, and subsequent incident reporting (internal and external). Thus, the cryptographic inventory provides broad benefits for today and tomorrow.

Cryptographic Use Cases

The cryptographic team conducts the inventory and analyses the results to create meaningful use cases to describe how the organization uses cryptography; the cryptographic inventory outputs are used in the risk analysis. The Canadian Forum for Digital Infrastructure Resilience (2023, 32) has identified 29 common cryptographic use cases and protocols (e.g., multifactor authentication, data at rest, and Kerberos authentication) for technical teams to get a quick start on their risk analysis. These detailed use cases are like templates that guide action to minimize risks and deliver the intended quality. These use cases may be applied during the design phase with the following structure:

1. Use case description,
2. Business value of the cryptography,
3. Prioritized data scope, volume, and lifespan,
4. Use case class (e.g., data in transit, data at rest, data in processing, digital signature),
5. Types of cryptography currently used,
6. Technical components (e.g., endpoints devices, networks, databases, file servers),
7. Cryptographic locations (e.g., DLL, hardware),
8. Technical dependencies for the use case affecting security,
9. Ability to support (pre- and post-quantum) cryptographic algorithms simultaneously within a hybrid cryptographic environment (e.g., consider interoperability and backward compatibility),
10. Risk analysis (probability of occurrence and impact—high, medium, or low).

The Canadian Forum for Digital Infrastructure Resilience (2023) document is an example of online resources to guide the IT and cybersecurity architects to develop and tailor cryptographic use cases as part of their risk analysis. Analyzing cryptographic use cases for risks and issues improves the probability of migration success. Project managers are advised to review technical resources to better comprehend the scope and complexity of cryptographic migrations, and to develop more accurate schedule and cost estimates, migration schedules, and project risk analyses. There will be *replace-or-update* decisions that will likely require new infrastructure (e.g., replace vulnerable IoT devices with post-quantum cryptographically resistant devices). The technical and cybersecurity teams will appreciate the project manager's familiarity with their technical domain leading to enhanced trust.

Quantum Cybersecurity Risk Treatment

Risk treatment (e.g., prevention and mitigation) involves progressing through a program of projects and initiatives toward the target state identified in the cybersecurity strategy. The cybersecurity target state includes goals such as (i) preventing the theft of sensitive data and information, (ii) ensuring transactional data is correct and not tampered with, (iii) preventing unauthorized access to digital systems, data, information, and so forth. It is worth repeating these goals in workshops and document them in formal project plans to build and maintain stakeholder alignment. Later, we review the post-quantum cryptographic risk analysis to identify which systems have sufficient post-quantum cryptography and which ones are susceptible to quantum risks.

Risk treatment follows and can be concurrent with iterations of risk identification and analysis during the inventory phase. The output of the inventory and its analysis is used to guide and prioritize quantum cybersecurity risk treatment. Indeed, the cybersecurity strategy may include preferred risk treatment options for classical and quantum risks and issues such as isolating and taking offline some of the organization's *crown jewels* and hardening its physical security to prevent unauthorized access. Some transfer risks to other parties (e.g., cybersecurity insurance). The project team benefits from following risk treatment processes and using templates and checklists to treat cryptographic and other risks (e.g., do nothing, update, or replace).

There is a variety of risk treatment options available to the organization and it is likely that multiple risk prevention and mitigation treatments are applied. The most common risk treatment options include:

Do nothing: There are some low-value systems, devices, and data that can be ignored due to the low impact of an attack using a classical or a cryptographically-relevant quantum computer. For example, some data are inherently low value or have a short expiration date where if that data were decrypted, the impact would be negligible. There may also be systems that are already protected from quantum risks as they are physically isolated or may have adequate cryptographic capabilities (e.g., sufficient symmetric and hash key sizes).

Update: Some systems and devices can be updated with quantum-resistant algorithms and technologies (e.g., replace digital signatures, keys, and asymmetric ciphers with NIST-recommended alternatives) and are the goal of post-quantum cryptography migration projects. Procurement teams are recommended to include post-quantum cryptographically friendly requirements for long term use technologies enabling cryptographic agility.

Replace: Some systems cannot accept post-quantum cryptography (e.g., unable to accommodate the new post-quantum cryptography due to technical constraints like limited key sizes). These systems will have to be replaced with post-quantum cryptographically secure technologies, then protected with approved post-quantum cryptographic algorithms. Some may use hybrid cryptography where post-quantum cryptography is used in conjunction with other forms of cryptography where increased robustness is required.

Isolate: Some data may be extremely sensitive (e.g., the organization's crown jewels) and may be taken offline to remove the risk of hacking with the goal to prevent unauthorized access (e.g., removed from the network including Wi-Fi networks). Organizations might isolate sensitive data until they are protected against the *steal now* risk.

Update, replace, and isolate are common risk treatment options the technical teams may consider and potentially use all three for different systems and data. There are also risk treatment options specific to quantum technologies for consideration.

Quantum Key Distribution

A promising but not yet broadly recommended approach to secure communications is the QKD network based on superposition. These are wired networks to create, protect, and transmit quantum and classical encryption keys between senders and receivers within the network. There are inherent limitations to QKD where repeaters are used to increase the distance between the sender and the receiver. Once these technologies are robust, a broad quantum internet may emerge. However, at this point in time, QKD solutions are not widely recommended (Australian Signals Directorate 2023; Canadian Centre for Cyber Security 2021; French Cybersecurity Agency 2020; British National Cyber Security Centre 2020; National Security Agency ND) and are therefore out of scope in this program management book.[§§] In the future, look for more QKD projects once the technology matures.

Quantum Random Number Generator

A quantum random number generator uses the unpredictability of quantum mechanics to generate truly random numbers (keys) that are theoretically impossible to predict and can be used to increase cryptographic encryption protection. It is possible to use quantum random number generators along with classical cryptography in a hybrid approach and may be explicitly addressed in the security policy and quantum cybersecurity strategy.

[§§] The authors are intrigued with and are following quantum key distribution research and development as progress is made to realizing the quantum internet: tomorrow's projects!

Post-Quantum Cryptography

One of the most recommended options to treat the risk of a cryptographically-relevant quantum computer used to break classical cryptography (e.g., RSA and Elliptic Curve Cryptography [ECC]) is to migrate to post-quantum cryptography (also known as quantum-proof, quantum-resistant, or quantum-safe cryptography). The target cryptographic environment will likely be a hybrid environment of classical and post-quantum cryptography. Post-quantum cryptography involves algorithms thought to be resistant against attacks from quantum and classical computers.

> All in all, post-quantum cryptography is less expensive, more flexible, and more mature than public key distribution. For these reasons, major security agencies do not support using quantum key distribution to secure communications and agree that post-quantum cryptography should be regarded as the best way to mitigate the quantum threat (TNO 2023, 11).

The IT and security architects can lead workshops to develop a post-quantum cryptographic migration and cutover strategy and plan to transition from quantum-susceptible cryptography to quantum-resistant cryptography where appropriate. A cryptography cutover strategy is a plan for a smooth transition from current cryptography (e.g., ECDSA) to post-quantum cryptography (e.g., FALCON) in the production environment. IT leadership will consider whether to replace or upgrade to quantum-secure cryptography and be informed by the cryptographic inventory results and cybersecurity strategy.

There have been previous cryptographic migrations to updated protocols; therefore, migration strategies are well understood, with a wealth of online resources related to planning and migration options (e.g., *big bang* or protocol by protocol migration). Analyzing, developing, and planning cryptographic migration strategies are left to the technical teams, and the technical guidance is out of scope for this project management book. However, technical teams will need time to work out detailed migration plans based on cryptographic dependencies and backward compatibility requirements (see Canadian Forum for Digital Infrastructure Resilience 2023, 64) about migration dependencies and cutover strategies. Understanding migration dependency and the cutover approach will help the project manager and team develop a feasible migration schedule with subsequent sprints.

The cybersecurity strategy can include a strategic goal to plan, budget, develop, maintain, and optimize robust testing capabilities and intelligent tools for the many quantum projects the organization will implement, including capabilities to evaluate and validate sophisticated post-quantum cryptographic interoperability and backward compatibility requirements that may be required for a decade or more. The IT and security architects and team will also develop and elaborate a cutover strategy to transition from the organization's current post-quantum cryptographic-susceptible to post-quantum cryptographic-resistant systems.

Again, there are extensive online resources to guide cryptographic migrations and cutover strategies and plans; the project manager may review some technical content to better understand post-quantum cryptographic migrations and hybrid cryptographic environments. Indeed, one can learn about best practices and risks and issues related to earlier cryptographic migrations (e.g., SHA-1 to SHA-2 hashes). The project manager, with a basic technical understanding, can collaborate and develop achievable project plans.

Post-quantum cryptography algorithms resistant to Shor's algorithm-based cyberattacks are designed to keep communications secure. A significant advantage of treating quantum cybersecurity risks with post-quantum cryptography is it can be *plugged into* classical cryptographic systems and devices (Joseph et al. 2022, 2380). Therefore, in *Quantum Cybersecurity*, our approach guides organizations to implement post-quantum cryptography aligned, tailored, and combined with best practices found in standards and frameworks.

Hybrid Cryptography

The risk treatment strategy may address the transition from classical only to hybrid cryptography (e.g., classical with quantum). Hybrid cryptography is an emerging concept where post-quantum cryptography is combined with another cryptographic system (e.g., classical) to achieve cryptographic diversity. When post-quantum cryptographic protection is combined with other protection methods, if one form of cryptography is compromised, another may continue to deliver protection. Apple's PQ3 protocol combines ECC with the CRYS-TALS–Kyber post-quantum encryption during the initial key establishment and later for rekeying. The PQ3 cryptography is *additive*; the hacker needs to defeat both the classical ECC and the post-quantum cryptography (Apple Security Research, 2024). Milestone watchers may interpret Apple's PQ3 messaging cryptography as another global leader committing to quantum.

The IT and security architects, and the data owners (e.g., business units), will determine the degree of cryptographic diversity since there is a trade-off where increased protection may result in increased demands on processing time, cost, bandwidth, upgrade complexity, and management. They may apply dual-signature or double-wrap solutions to the organization's most critical data as part of the migration program. Or generate truly random keys with a quantum random number generator to add increased protection. The IT and security architects will create a program of projects to progress to their target state that likely includes hybrid cryptography. The IT and security architects will benefit from additional time and support to consider hybrid cryptography since hybrid cryptography planning, design, testing, and implementation is "a very complex topic from a cryptoanalysis and implementation perspectives" (Canadian Forum for Digital Infrastructure Resilience 2023, 55).

Minimum Viable Cybersecurity Foundation

The initial set of projects (e.g., large scale) and initiatives (e.g., small scale) an organization should implement if they have not already done so to protect themselves from the *steal now, decrypt later* attack. The organization may also implement cybersecurity projects to comply with maturing government regulations and accrediting requirements. The organization may refer to the NIST tiers and controls to progress to a minimum viable cybersecurity foundation. The inventory will provide current state cryptographic information and the gap analysis will help identify and prioritize the security requirements and projects to mature to the target state: a minimum viable cybersecurity foundation as represented by the Australia's *Essential Eight* or CISA's *Cybersecurity Performance Goals*. Some of these projects may be nontechnical such as cybersecurity process improvement (e.g., integrate and practice the detect, respond, and recover playbooks) and upskilling to prepare for post-quantum cryptographic migrations. Therefore, establishing a minimum viable cybersecurity foundation (including people, process, and technology dimensions) that protects against steal now, decrypt later risks will likely be the priority for many organizations.

No-Regret Cybersecurity Projects

Another category of projects is no-regret cybersecurity projects: implementing cybersecurity components that benefit the organization no matter what direction the digital landscape takes. For example, an organization might strengthen its cyber incident reporting capabilities ahead of anticipated regulatory changes; indeed, executive leadership and corporate boards increasingly desire timely enterprise risk management reports.

Cryptographic Agility

> *The ability of an organization to react to changes in the cryptographic landscape requires knowledge of all uses of cryptography across its businesses. It is broader than just the encryption keys and algorithms and must also include the underlying technology and business processes that are being supported* (FS-ISAC 2023a, 5).

There are two cryptographic agility goals with project implications: (i) stop (or at least minimize) procuring any technologies that cannot be upgraded to post-quantum cryptography and (ii) develop, maintain, and continually improve the ability to quickly respond to changes in cryptographic requirements. Without this agility, the organization may struggle to secure its data and systems from a quantum-enabled cyberattack. The first round of NIST-endorsed algorithms will be implemented without actual testing with a cryptographically-relevant quantum computer; the algorithms were endorsed by NIST *before* the arrival of a cryptographically-relevant quantum computer. Therefore, there is a risk that some algorithms may have vulnerabilities that are exposed in real quantum attacks and may be protected with subsequent post-quantum cryptographic updates.

Cryptographic agility can be enhanced by stopping the procurement of noncryptographically agile products. The procurement policy and procedures can include cryptographic agility clauses in requests for information and proposal documents, as well as contracts, to assure new technology is cryptographically agile and will not have to be replaced in future migrations.

Achieving cryptographic agility has implications beyond procurement:

> Implementing strong key management procedures, updating cryptographic protocols and technologies, and providing training and resources to ensure that staff members are knowledgeable about both established and new cryptographic technologies are just a few examples of the various activities that can go into achieving crypto agility (FS-ISAC 2023a, 10).

Therefore, cryptographic agility goes beyond a technology perspective and involves a broad range of technical and nontechnical projects and initiatives.

Quantum Readiness Maturity

The concept of maturity has been widely adopted (e.g., in software engineering and project management) and is hinted at in the NIST Cybersecurity Framework (e.g., tiers) as it is recognized as a best practice when tailored and combined properly. Therefore, for the organization to be quantum-ready, it will have a continual improvement culture where cybersecurity maturity is purposely pursued through strategic projects and initiatives. Therefore, the target state encompasses a continual flow of people, processes, and technology projects and initiatives to support cybersecurity readiness. As you can see, there are many quantum-related projects to manage and govern to transition to a state of cybersecurity readiness (e.g., post-quantum cryptography and cryptographic agility). These planned series of transitions to reach the target state is the essence of maturity models and applicable to guide organizations to optimized digital environments.

Thus, risk treatment follows risk identification: organizations create a cryptographic inventory, analyze, and prioritize their risks (and gaps), then implement treatment projects and initiatives like quantum awareness and post-quantum cryptographic migrations. At its core, organizations face a massive undertaking of projects, and aligning, tailoring, and combining best practices found in standards and frameworks improve the probability of program and project success. A major element of risk management is governance: monitor and control the quantum strategies and the program of projects and initiatives.

Governance

Governance is a central function in project, service, and cybersecurity management as they are positioned as critical success factors:

> The creation of the strategy is not a one-off activity and cannot be expressed as a single document that is then never amended. Strategy is not destination: it is a journey with a stated direction and objectives. Therefore, strategy management activities are ongoing (AXELOS 2020, 66).

As strategy is ongoing, so is its related governance. The main governance actions in service management are to direct, monitor, and evaluate that the strategy is implemented as planned (AXELOS 2020, 31) and are incorporated in our hybrid project management approach used in *Quantum Cybersecurity*. The updated NIST Cybersecurity Framework outlines mature cybersecurity governance capabilities (NIST 2024, 25):

- The organization has a holistic and comprehensive approach to cybersecurity risk management including policies, processes, and procedures to address potential cybersecurity risks,
- Cybersecurity risks and organizational objectives are linked and considered during the decision-making process,
- Senior executives and business unit leadership in mature organizations manage cybersecurity risks like financial and other significant enterprise risks,
- The cybersecurity budget is risk-based to address current and future risk treatment requirements.

It is within this enterprise risk management context that quantum awareness is spread, risks are managed, and governance is improved. The reader is invited to review program management governance (PMI 2017, Figure 1.1) and its key domains (PMI 2017, 25) and to adapt and tailor governance practices throughout the quantum program of projects:

Program strategy alignment: Align the quantum program outcomes and objectives with the organization's quantum goals and objectives. When developing program plans, compare them to the business, IT, and cybersecurity strategies to check for alignment. Tables and spreadsheets are useful to display alignment.

Program benefits management: Define, create, maximize, and deliver the benefits provided by the quantum program. The ITIL Framework can be tailored for quantum-related benefits management as the *value* of the quantum service is identified, implemented, used, optimized, and tracked. It is the responsibility of the service owner to measure the benefits provided through a program of projects; the project manager is responsible for project success, and the project sponsor (also known as the service owner in ITIL terminology) is responsible for measuring the benefits of the product or service derived through the program of projects and initiatives. The product or service delivered through the project or sprint is called deliverables in PMBOK® Guide nomenclature.

Program stakeholder engagement: Identify and analyze the quantum stakeholder needs and manage their expectations beginning with quantum awareness projects and initiatives.

Program governance: Establish a framework for decision making that supports and maintains quantum program oversight through to program closure. The PMO is well-positioned to facilitate program governance and support optimization projects or initiatives to streamline program and project decision making.

The project manager and quantum program sponsors collaboratively and iteratively plan the quantum program; however, the quantum technologies subject matter experts guide technical activities like designing and testing. Program governance, like cybersecurity, in essence, is risk management.

Risk Management

Risk management is at the core of cybersecurity, program, project, and service management and is reflected in standards and frameworks. In *Quantum Cybersecurity*, we combine and tailor our hybrid project management approach to align with best practices to provide a risk-based approach to quantum technology and cybersecurity projects (Figure 3.9).

The pathway to quantum technology adoption begins with developing strategies for the organization (business strategy), technological infrastructure (information technology systems, information systems, and industrial control systems), and to secure the organization's data and systems against a cryptographically-relevant quantum computer (cybersecurity strategy). Inherent in strategy is to identify and treat the risks related to achieving

Figure 3.9 Quantum best practices alignment

the strategy. As quantum technologies and cybersecurity are digital, we align with the ITIL Framework and its Strategy Management practice to develop and manage strategy including governance.

A fundamental risk identification task is to conduct a cryptographic inventory as recommended by NIST (2023c, 2). The reader can conduct at least two risk analyses: first, analyze quantum risks as per standard risk management practices outlined in the PMBOK® Guide or ISO/IEC 31001 Risk Assessment (Figure 3.5). Second, analyze the organization's risks related to the arrival of a cryptographically-relevant quantum computer with Mosca's Theorem (Figure 3.8). Risk analysis informs the risk treatment process resulting in a comprehensive program of projects to treat quantum cybersecurity risks and system vulnerabilities (people, process, and technology). Organizations follow best practices (NIST 2020b), manage risks, and regularly use a risk and issue register, and all of which contribute to good governance.

Security Policies and Procedures

Governance is enhanced with policies and procedures to guide decision making. It is best practice for organizations to maintain security policies and procedures that detail their acceptable cryptography, key sizes, algorithms, and so forth. Guidelines for cryptographic agility for procured technology may form part of the updated technology procurement policy and procedures. A benefit of cryptographic policy and procedures is they can reduce the inflow of post-quantum crypto-graphically susceptible technology that can add to future migration efforts. Reviewing and updating security policies and procedures can be added to the quantum product backlog for early prioritization and sprint execution (Figure 2.10). Policies and procedures are not only governance critical success factors, but they are also quality assurance guidelines that direct behavior to reduce risks and deliver the intended quality in the program of quantum projects and initiatives.

Quantum Champions

The organization will benefit from a champion role to prepare the organization to adopt quantum technologies and to transition to post-quantum readiness. The champion role will likely be shared among technical and nontechnical leaders like yourself. Quantum champions perform many duties, such as raising awareness, developing strategic plans, creating program roadmaps, monitoring quantum trends and milestones, encouraging quantum technologies and algorithms experimentation, and engaging with internal and external stakeholders.

The quantum champion may collaborate with the organization's risk, legal, and compliance specialists to reduce quantum-related risks and issues. For example, the quantum champion may collaborate with the risk auditing team to identify and analyze quantum risks (internal and external). Those organizations applying enterprise risk management may also add quantum risks and issues to their program. A key governance goal is to ensure cryptographic agility is designed into each technical solution and application.

A quantum champion pursues organizational change management. Change management has a long tradition, and we leave it to the reader to discover the works of Rosabeth Moss Kanter and John Kotter and adopt techniques like those in the Prosci ADKAR® Model.

To conclude, in Chapter 3, we introduced quantum strategies for business, IT, and cybersecurity that form the basis for a quantum program of projects and initiatives. The quantum business strategy outlines the organization's vision for quantum technologies. Business unit leadership develops digital use cases that are part of the larger quantum business case and are submitted for funding and approval. The IT strategy supports the business strategy and direction. The quantum cybersecurity strategy protects the organization's sensitive data and systems as the organization progresses.

For a successful implementation and adoption of quantum projects, there are at least two succinct critical success factors: *the right projects, done right* (as proclaimed by Paul Dinsmore and Terry Cooke-Davies). These two critical success factors are related to getting the right quantum strategies for the organization, and then successfully implementing the program of quantum projects and initiatives to achieve these strategies. In *Quantum Cybersecurity Program Management*, we align with project and program standards from the Project Management Institute, and frameworks like the NIST Cybersecurity Framework and the ITIL Service Management Framework. Add the *Goldilocks Approach* to adopt, tailor, and combine just the right amount of standards and frameworks to arrive at a lean and hybrid approach to quantum project management. In Chapter 4, we introduce quantum cybersecurity program management to deliver business, technology, and cybersecurity strategies.

Microlearning

More resources can be found online about quantum strategies and change management:

- Learn more about how NIST Cybersecurity Framework governance categories and subcategories contribute to governance,
- Find program and project governance templates and checklists to add to your quantum projects including those in the design phase,
- Learn about how AI is used to improve governance,
- Discover how PMOs are implementing quantum technologies relevant to your industry and discipline,
- Locate best practices for quantum champions (e.g., Kotter's 8-Steps),
- Download the *Standard for Change Management and ACMP Change Management Code of Ethics* from The Association of Change Management Professionals (ACMP).

CHAPTER 4

Quantum Program Management

To deliver a series of diverse quantum projects (people, process, and technology), program management best practices can be the guide. Program management is about managing projects collectively to extract benefits not available through individual project management. The *Standard for Program Management* from the Project Management Institute is the foundation for this book. We propose a program of projects and initiatives (smaller projects) to develop cryptographic agility and implement post-quantum cryptography. While ITIL has the Portfolio Management practice, we defer to the comprehensive standards from the Project Management Institute (e.g., *A Guide to the Project Management Body of Knowledge, The Standard for Program Management,* and the *Agile Practice Guide*).

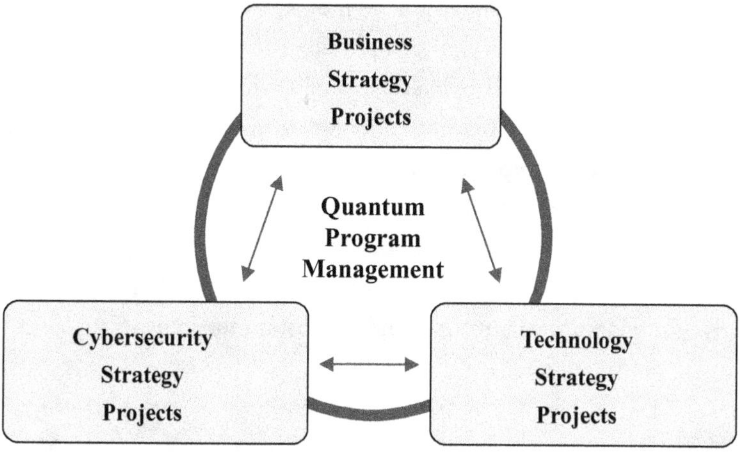

Figure 4.1 ITIL strategy governance

Strategy Implementation Through Program Management

Business, technology, and cybersecurity strategies guide program management (Figure 4.1). For each strategy, there will be a series of projects (Figure 2.5) implemented to achieve their strategic objectives (e.g., target state). These projects include the following:

Cybersecurity foundation projects: to protect against steal now, decrypt later risks,

Quantum awareness projects: to prepare the organization's people and external partners and vendors to adopt quantum technologies and to implement post-quantum cryptography and other risk treatment measures,

Quantum business case projects: to implement quantum technologies and applications for business use (e.g., quantum technologies applied to manufacturing optimization),

Project management optimization projects: to tailor a project management delivery approach for the many cybersecurity projects and initiatives to follow,

Service management optimization projects and initiatives: to tailor an end-to-end service management approach to support the quantum technology and cybersecurity work to come,

Cryptographic agility projects: (i) to ensure the digital ecosystem becomes post-quantum cryptographically *compliant* and no new post-quantum cryptographically *vulnerable* technologies are introduced and (ii) to maintain and optimize cryptographic agility should the need arise to migrate to updated cryptography,

Post-quantum cryptography projects and initiatives: to migrate to post-quantum resistant cybersecurity protocols,

Quantum enabling projects and initiatives: to support the quantum program such as providing university scholarships for quantum technologies and internships for students to aid recruitment efforts.

Therefore, quantum stakeholders can align their quantum strategies and deliver strategic objectives with a program management approach to reduce risks and deliver the right level of quality.

Project Prioritization

Selecting projects[*] and initiatives is guided by the business, IT, and cybersecurity strategies. The organization selects and prioritizes quantum-related initiatives and projects, and IT leadership manages the demand for these approved projects. One of the early decisions regards the sequence of projects and initiatives, in essence program management. In *Quantum Cybersecurity*, we recommend treating any severe risks related to the steal now, decrypt later attack a priority and as part of the minimum viable cybersecurity foundation projects.

Quantum Program Management

The vast majority of quantum readiness steps are typically incremental steps on existing business as well as technical, strategic and operational processes and procedures (Canadian Forum for Digital Infrastructure Resilience 2023, 94).

Often code words are used when quantum program management is discussed; for example, *incremental steps* may be *sprints*, and *challenges* and *threats* may be *risks* and *issues*. Therefore, a careful reading of the literature reveals recommendations for a risk-based and program management approach, aligned with best practices found in standards

---

[*] While it is convention to use the term *project selection*, we believe it is erroneous. Organizations do not select projects; rather, they approve and fund products and services that contribute to the organization's mission and objectives. An analogy is we don't want the three-year-long construction site (project); we want the affordable housing community (project deliverable or product of the project). Organizations do not want the post-quantum cryptographic migrations instead, they want the security brought about through implementing post-quantum cryptographic algorithms to provide an agile cryptographic environment.

Planning and Governance										

Quantum Technologies and Cybersecurity Awareness										

Risk Identification and Analysis

Cryptographic Inventory	○ ○ ○ ○	○ ○
Risk Prioritization	○ ○ ○ ○ ○ ○ ○	

Risk Treatment/Response Projects

Cybersecurity Foundation (e.g., CISA *Cybersecurity Performance Goals*)	○ ○ ○ ○ ○
Cryptographic Agility	○ ○ ○ ○ ○ ○ ○
Service Management Foundation	○ ○ ○ ○ ○ ○
Project Management Foundation	○ ○ ○ ○ ○ ○
Quantum Technologies (H/W and S/W)	○ ○ ○ ○ ○ ○
Cryptographic Migrations	○ ○ ○ ○ ○ ○ ○ ○ ○ ○ ○

years   3   6   9

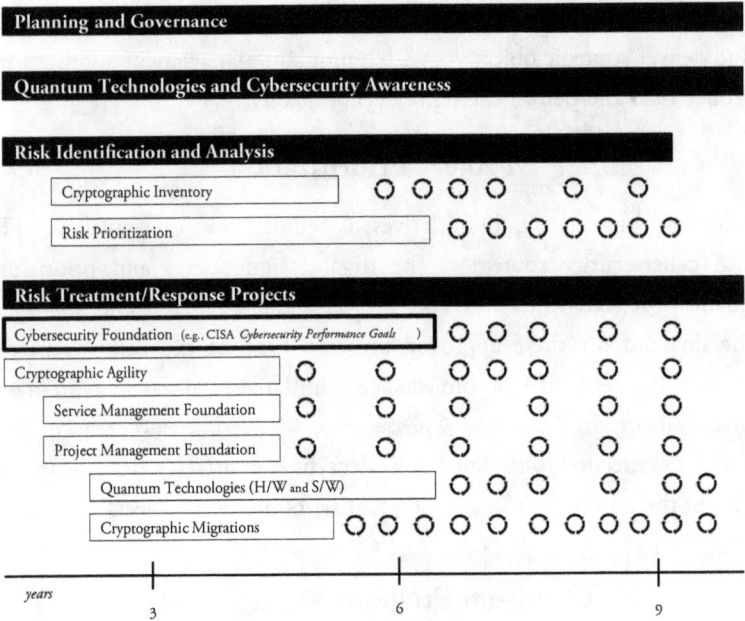

Figure 4.2 Quantum program Gantt chart

and frameworks to transition to quantum technologies and post-quantum cryptography. However, the diversity of concurrent and consecutive projects is perhaps daunting leaving the quantum project manager uncertain where to begin. We outline a program of quantum projects, including post-quantum cryptography projects (Figure 4.2).

Cybersecurity foundation projects provide essential cybersecurity including preventing the *steal now* element of the steal now, decrypt later risk and should be prioritized to protect the organization's sensitive information. IT leadership may also stop procuring technologies that cannot be upgraded to post-quantum cryptography and thereby reduce cryptographic agility risks. Once the initial projects to guard against steal now, decrypt later attacks have been initiated, and cryptographic agility is addressed, the organization can fine-tune its project and technology service management processes, training, tools, checklists, and templates to guide a decade's worth of quantum projects to come.

Organizations also begin quantum awareness projects and initiatives that will lead to business use-case discovery, experimentation, and development (e.g., projects). Awareness projects include working with internal and external stakeholders to develop and follow a pathway leading to post-quantum cryptography and cryptographic agility. Any approved quantum business use cases (e.g., new quantum software for the finance unit) can be scheduled for implementation, triggering quantum technology projects (e.g., hardware, software, integration).

A critical group of projects is the cryptographic inventory (e.g., risk identification and analysis) followed by post-quantum cryptographic migration projects (e.g., risk treatment). Continual improvement sprints (e.g., initiatives) follow quantum projects (Figure 2.10). Not included in the quantum Gantt chart (Figure 4.2) are other quantum-supporting projects like judging students' projects at a school science fair. Thus, the quantum program of projects begins with addressing any significant cybersecurity gaps to establish a solid foundation for the organization's cybersecurity.

Cybersecurity Foundation Projects

It is imperative to protect the organization's sensitive data and systems from the steal now, decrypt later risks and to build a minimum viable cybersecurity foundation through projects and continual improvement initiatives. These quantum cybersecurity projects include protecting today's data in use, at rest, and in transit from future quantum decryption actions. The daily flow of an organization's data through the public internet to an off-site backup location is an example of sensitive data in transit at risk. Indeed, there are common cybersecurity misconfigurations (e.g., poor patch management) that are used by hackers to exploit system vulnerabilities and these misconfigurations can be reviewed as part of risk identification (NSA and CISA 2023). Therefore, organizations are advised to harden current systems aligned with best practices such as Australia's *Essential Eight* or CISA's *Cybersecurity Performance Goals*. For example, the cybersecurity team can implement sprints to increase Rivest–Shamir–Adleman (RSA) key sizes to reduce brute force attacks or increase higher-bit hash sizes to SHA-512, for example (Palo Alto Networks LTD 2023, 8). While a solid cybersecurity foundation is being implemented, maintained, and optimized, the organization can raise awareness for the dual potentialities of quantum technologies.

Microlearning

Establishing a minimum viable cybersecurity foundation, then maintaining, and optimizing those services is necessary for quantum cybersecurity readiness; how can an organization expect to protect its systems and most sensitive data from complex quantum cybersecurity risks without the cybersecurity basics? Therefore, find out more about:

- Minimum viable cybersecurity recommendations for your industry and related regulations,
- The Australian Signals Directorate's *Information Security Manual* (e.g., Planning for Post-quantum Cryptography Standards),
- Cybersecurity self-assessments to determine the current state.

Quantum Awareness Projects

An early series of projects and initiatives in the quantum technologies program is to develop awareness, enthusiasm, and commitment (e.g., sustainable funding), followed by quantum-related skills development or acquisition. Given the criticality and complexity of the quantum program, we recommend formally initiating awareness projects and applying just the right amount of project management—the *Goldilocks Principle*. The awareness goals include setting up the initial quantum transition team, estimating the scope of the quantum program of projects including rough order of magnitude estimates for the budget and schedule timelines (e.g., a program Gantt chart; see Figure 4.2), and engaging stakeholders. The quantum champion might take a survey or inventory of other like-minded colleagues to assist with subsequent quantum technology projects and change management.

The reader may find there are equally enthusiastic people in their organization willing to join the quantum transition team, through to people who have never heard about quantum technologies, let alone the existential risk a cryptographically-relevant quantum computer may present to the organization. The team will often begin with just one person, but can expand and include:

- Executive leadership sponsor to support and maintain the momentum toward quantum program targets,
- Quantum project manager (e.g., tasked with the role to create awareness in the organization) who may oversee all or parts of the program of projects,
- Quantum champions (e.g., you; there can be many!) to spark awareness, enthusiasm, and commitment for perhaps a decade of quantum projects,
- Quantum subject matter experts (SMEs) and quantum technologies end users within the discipline (e.g., finance, manufacturing, pharmaceutical research and development, engineering) will collaborate with IT to develop quantum technology use cases and eventually submit quantum technology business cases for funding and approval,
- Quantum cybersecurity SMEs will monitor cybersecurity trends and make recommendations for the organization. Nontechnical cybersecurity SMEs mostly specialize in the govern, identify, and protect functions (and the focus of this book), while technical cybersecurity SMEs specialize in the detect, respond, and recover functions detailed in the NIST Cybersecurity Framework,
- IT SMEs (e.g., IT architect, integration specialist),
- Supporting SMEs (e.g., procurement, legal and compliance, recruiting, training, CapEx/OpEx budgeting),
- External stakeholders (e.g., partners, vendors, third parties, clients, customers, consultants).

There are likely other specialized quantum roles that may benefit organizations. Indeed, a person may find themselves in multiple roles (e.g., quantum champion and project manager).

There are at least three major categories of stakeholders who can benefit from early quantum technologies and cybersecurity awareness: (i) IT leadership including those in the PMO, operations, information security, infrastructure, integration, and so forth, (ii) business leadership

Table 4.1 Awareness recommendations for leadership

Learn About ...	Take Action ...
• The dual potentialities of quantum technologies and their impacts on businesses • Legal and regulatory implications of quantum technologies • Risk treatment options like post-quantum cryptography and migrations • Best practices in managing organizational change (e.g., Prosci ADKAR method) and best practices in project and technology service management (e.g., ITIL)	• To establish a minimum viable cybersecurity foundation if not already achieved • To develop a holistic approach (people, process, and technology) to adopt quantum technologies and balance protection from quantum risks, with organizational agility • To invest in updating and replacing susceptible with resistant post-quantum cryptographic systems • To prioritize and include cryptographic agility in procurement practices • To hire and train knowledgeable staff in both the IT and end-user departments • To coordinate both internally and externally to develop a program plan to transition to quantum technologies

and users of the quantum applications, and (iii) external partners, vendors, and customers who are part of your quantum ecosystem (upstream and downstream). Look for quantum champions in these three stakeholder categories to collaborate and participate in quantum awareness projects and related training.

A goal of awareness is to secure sustained executive support and resource commitment if it is not already achieved. The executive leadership support allows the quantum transition team to proceed with resources and approval to bring the organization into a quantum ecosystem and to protect against the risks posed by threat actors with a cryptographically-relevant quantum computer. There are early awareness actions (adapted from the World Economic Forum 2022b, 21–22) for leadership including board members, and cybersecurity leadership (Tables 4.1 and 4.2).

Cybersecurity leadership, if they have not already done so, can also quickly learn about quantum technologies and cybersecurity and the

Table 4.2 Awareness recommendations for cybersecurity leadership

Learn About ...	Take Action ...
• Relevant government regulations, industry accreditations • Quantum technologies milestones including when a cryptographically-relevant quantum computer becomes available and powerful enough to break classical cryptography (e.g., the Z in Mosca's Theorem) • The others in your organization who are keen to be quantum early adopters and future collaborators	• To spread awareness up, down, in, and outside of your organization to leverage quantum opportunities and to implement post-quantum cryptographic resistant risk treatment projects • To conduct quantum-related risk analyses (both positive and negative risks) • To plan and implement a cryptographic inventory followed by risk analysis and treatment

distinct actions they can take (Table 4.2). Quantum awareness campaigns and mentoring by a quantum champion (guided by Tables 4.1 and 4.2) can expedite quantum awareness, enthusiasm, and commitment.

Quantum awareness is facilitated by aligning to standards (e.g., PMBOK® Guide) and frameworks (e.g., NIST Cybersecurity Framework and ITIL Service Management) since they provide common terminology, tools, processes, and theory; all of which provide the opportunity for a shared understanding. Indeed, these standards and frameworks are globally adopted. Therefore, we endeavor to align with terminology in de facto global standards and frameworks in our approach to quantum cybersecurity program management.

Beyond awareness is developing or attracting quantum competencies. Guided by Bloom's taxonomy of cognitive thought (e.g., how learning progresses from simple to complex thought), organizations can first provide knowledge about quantum technologies, use cases, and cybersecurity to orient the organization. To innovate and protect with quantum technologies, many of the organization's people will need to progress through Bloom's Taxonomy levels (Figure 4.3) to learn about these new technologies in order to develop quantum technologies use cases. A common upskilling model is the ADDIE model of Instructional Design where the instructional designer analyses learning requirements and designs, develops, and implements training, followed by training and learning evaluation.

Organizations can benefit from a formal approach to upskilling to prepare for the adoption and optimization of quantum computing technologies and use cases; however, detailing quantum awareness and training projects are out of our scope as there are online resources. We also direct the reader to *Cybersecurity Training: A Pathway to Readiness* (Skulmoski and Walker 2023) to learn about a project-oriented approach to cybersecurity training and awareness including recommendations to establish quantum communities of practice.

Quantum Cybersecurity, Cybersecurity Training (people), and *Shields Up* (process and technology) work together for a comprehensive approach to technology project management and continual improvement aligned with global standards and frameworks. These books can be part of the quantum awareness program for the decade of projects and upskilling to come.

Project Management Optimization Projects

Another early project to undertake ahead of the main body of quantum cybersecurity work (e.g., a cryptographic inventory and post-quantum cryptographic migrations) is to optimize the relevant processes and tools. Organizations can reduce risks and deliver the right level of quality with lean project delivery approaches supported by processes (e.g., risk management), templates (e.g., migration plan), checklists (e.g., post-quantum cryptography validation), and training (e.g., applying the organization's project management approach, tools, and processes to post-quantum cryptographic migrations). We are reminded of the master woodcutter (and American politician, Abraham Lincoln) who wrote: "Give me six hours to chop down a tree and I will spend the first four sharpening the axe." Therefore, optimizing project management can improve project delivery quality and reduce risks.

Leadership can review the Project Management Institute's Organizational Project Management Maturity Model to evaluate their level of maturity and guide their optimization projects and initiatives.[†] Many project management optimizations (e.g., creating a post-quantum

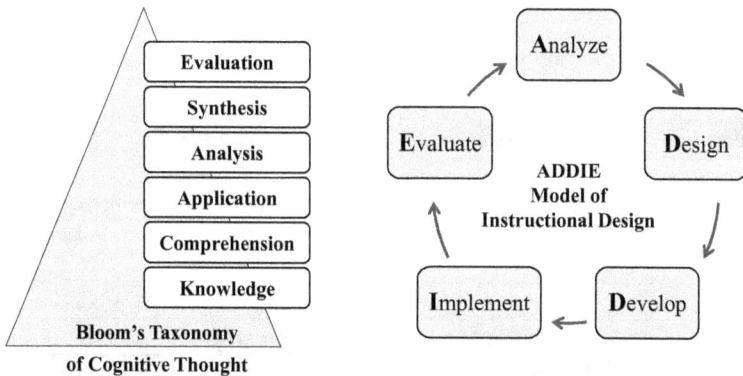

Figure 4.3 Quantum awareness and training foundation

cryptography go-live checklist) can be delivered through initiatives rather than the more formal and comprehensive hybrid project approach. Organizations can align project (and service) management with sustainable development goals (e.g., fairness) along with project management effectiveness and efficiency goals (GPM 2023, 6).

Service Management Optimization Projects

As organizations review and optimize project management, they can also review and optimize service management for the decade of quantum projects to follow. Again, organizations benefit from reusing tools and processes like conducting a gap analysis for their service (technology) management capabilities. During design phase workshops, the teams may identify service management optimization opportunities that can be delivered by judiciously applying and tailoring ITIL practices, combined with other standards and frameworks (Table 4.3 as an example; however, as organizations are unique, their minimum viable foundations may vary, and different standards and frameworks may be substituted). The goal is to provide a minimum viable service management foundation as new quantum and classical computing products and services are released into the production environment and old technologies are disposed.

The minimum viable suite of standards and frameworks for implementing quantum technology projects can be combined and

Table 4.3 Minimum viable quantum management best practices example

Phase	Standards and Frameworks (Partial List)
Strategy	ITIL Strategy Management practice, NIST Cybersecurity Framework, PMI Standard for Program Management, NIST IR 8286 Integrating Cybersecurity and Enterprise Risk Management, change management (e.g., Prosci ADKAR, Kotter's 8-Steps)
Initiate	ITIL Service Request Management practice, PMI PMBOK® Guide
Plan	ITIL Portfolio Management practice, PMI PMBOK® Guide
Design	ITIL Service Design practice, NIST Cybersecurity Framework, NIST Special Publication 1800-38B Migration to Post-Quantum Cryptography Quantum Readiness: Cryptographic Discovery Volume B: Approach, Architecture, and Security Characteristics of Public Key Application Discovery Tools
Build	ITIL Service Configuration Management practice
Quality control	ITIL Service Validation and Testing practice, NIST Special Publication 1800-38C Migration to Post-Quantum Cryptography Quantum Readiness: Testing Draft Standards
T2P and Go-live	ITIL Release Management, Deployment Management, Service Catalog, Incident Management practices
Others	ISO 31000 Risk Management, ISO 9001 Quality Management, ITIL Continual Improvement practice
IT operations	PMI Agile Practice Guide, ITIL service management practices

tailored to fit the organization's requirements and levels of maturity. Since organizations are unique, the minimum viable service management configuration varies, and the *Goldilocks* sweet spot is pursued, maintained, and optimized through continual improvement iterations. Some organizations may need more or fewer processes and tools and will tune them for quantum technologies. Additional quality assurance is added with training and practice prior to migrating post-quantum cryptography to the production environment or disposing of legacy assets. Recall the value proposition of standards and frameworks is if judiciously applied, tailored, and optimized, risks are reduced, and the intended quality objectives are more likely to be achieved.

Each technology and cybersecurity project may also include standard processes, templates, and checklists like updating the service catalog and configuration management register. These administrative tasks are often part of the transition to production (T2P) process, and some can be completed prior to the T2P phase. Maintaining up-to-date documentation is a common element in standards and frameworks and the ITIL Framework includes practices to guide documentation.

When designing processes, the IT and security architects might review operational service management processes and tune them for the go-live through to end-of-service phases. For example, since some devices may need to be replaced, rather than upgraded, the technology disposal phase can be included in end-to-end process reviews. The end-to-end technology service management processes may be reviewed during the design phase and prior to implementing a major technology refresh. ITIL's IT Asset Management practice includes best practices for IT asset disposal. Many of the service management optimizations (e.g., creating a legacy technology disposal checklist) can be delivered through month-long initiatives. Sustainable asset disposal processes and other service management processes can be tuned for quantum technology projects.

Quantum Business Case Projects

A major group of projects in the quantum program is related to enabling business use cases. Business leadership will learn about quantum technologies benefits and start envisioning about the possibilities they can bring to their departments. Quantum champions will pursue and experiment with innovative products and services enabled by quantum technologies. These champions may not be experts in quantum technologies and will want to collaborate with technical teams. That collaboration can be energized and strengthened by aligning

---

† A misconception about maturity models is the user needs to implement the entire maturity model to derive benefits from its value proposition (reduce risks and achieve the desired level of quality). However, maturity models are meant to be tailored to the needs of the organization (unless there is a regulatory compliance requirement). Therefore, organizations choose just the right amount of the maturity model as in the *Goldilocks Principle*. Greg Skulmoski served on the Project Management Institute's first *Organizational Project Model Maturity Model* project and applied and tailored its best practices to quantum technologies program management.

with service and project management practices and developing business quantum use cases (Table 3.1) for consideration. Approved quantum business cases will likely require quantum technologies (e.g., hardware, software, devices, and integration) and may be delivered through projects and initiatives.

Quantum Technology Projects and Initiatives

As always, there is a continuous flow of technology projects and initiatives; now, there are requests for quantum technologies including subject matter expertise (people), integration, hardware and devices, and software to support quantum business case implementation. There may be requests for quantum and classical technologies to support and automate post-quantum cryptographic migrations (e.g., upgrade APIs to allow easy updates to cryptographic primitives and algorithms, replace key management software). Indeed, providing the infrastructure for these projects will account for a considerable amount of project effort and organizational resources (Joseph 2022, 241).

To manage requests for technology, including quantum technologies, the ITIL Service Value System begins with the demand for technology (Figures 2.1 and 2.2). The brilliance of the ITIL Framework (and the PMBOK® Guide) is it applies to managing most technologies, most of the time. Therefore, organizations can reduce risks and deliver the right level of quality by applying, tailoring, and combining the ITIL Service Management Framework and standards from the Project Management Institute in their quantum projects and initiatives (Figure 2.14). In *Shields Up: Cybersecurity Project Management*, we detail a hybrid approach to delivering technology projects, including cybersecurity, that is aligned with NIST frameworks and special publications, the ITIL Framework and PMI standards that the reader may review. Therefore, in the quantum program of projects, there will be a coordinated stream of projects to build a quantum technologies ecosystem and capabilities.

Cryptographic Agility Projects

In the quantum program, there will be projects to replace or update system components to foster cryptographic agility. Cryptographic agility is the ability to respond to cryptographic changes efficiently and effectively (e.g., the goal is to minimize the security risk, disruption, time, cost, and resources to change cryptography). A major goal of cryptographic agility is the ability to respond and resist new attacks. The cryptographic agility strategy is led and developed by the security and IT architects and may result in new technical design requirements to maintain the organization's minimum viable cybersecurity foundation resulting in additional projects and initiatives. When planning for cryptographic agility (Canadian Forum for Digital Infrastructure Resilience 2023, 10):

- Work with procurement to adopt modular designs so it is easier to make changes (e.g., algorithm independence of technology),
- Implement flexible API technologies that allow for easy updates to cryptographic primitives and algorithms,
- Provide nimble key management systems to generate, store, update, and rotate cryptographic keys of different types and lengths,
- Adopt standardized cryptographic solutions (e.g., algorithms) where possible and monitor changes to standards and frameworks should there be an urgent need to upgrade cryptography to more secure versions,
- Apply best practices like lean cybersecurity including post-quantum cryptographic documentation, training, testing, and auditing. Review and revise the organization's cyber incident plans (e.g., respond and recover also known as resilience) and cryptographic changes. Update the ITIL strategic plan based on the audit.

The project manager, IT, and security architects can plan, prioritize, and coordinate projects and initiatives that contribute to cryptographic agility and strengthen the organization's current and future cybersecurity foundation. Indeed, the concept of agility is expanding beyond project management to IT architectural agility, data agility, technology agility, process agility, career agility, and business agility. The leadership team is encouraged to discuss agility broadly during quantum strategy development and program planning to investigate other nimble options that contribute to quantum safety and security.

Microlearning

While the variety of quantum-related projects is wide, more resources can be found online:

- Latest trends in technology service management including optimization and minimum viable foundation best practices, documentation, and service management automation,
- The transformation of project management and PMOs due to emerging technologies like AI, big data, and quantum technologies,
- Best practices and risks related to cryptographic agility.

Post-Quantum Cryptographic Migration Projects

Most organizations will implement post-quantum cryptographic migration projects. Simply, these projects update or replace *vulnerable* with post-quantum cryptographic *resistant* algorithms to keep systems and sensitive data safe and secure. The cryptographic migration target and approach will be designed by the organization's technical teams with input from project management colleagues (e.g., scoping, scheduling, managing risks). The scope of these migration projects is vast and complex since the encryption currently used in classical computing is pervasive, layered, heterogeneous, and sometimes hidden. Therefore, there will be a continuous stream of post-quantum cryptographic migration projects and initiatives to update and replace cryptography in the organization's digital ecosystem (internal and external). There is also the risk that the first version of post-quantum cryptographic algorithms may have vulnerabilities necessitating additional cryptographic updates (e.g., migrations). The degree or maturity of the organization's cryptographic agility will influence the cryptography update timelines, risks, and the probability of update project success.

NIST announced the first quantum-resistant cryptographic algorithms after a six-year competition: CRYSTALS–Kyber, CRYS-TALS–Dilithium, SPHINCS+, and FALCON. The first three have been released with draft standards with a FALCON draft standard to follow. It is expected that these algorithms will be adopted through post-quantum cryptographic migrations.

Post-Quantum Cryptographic Migration Quality Assurance

A quantum program goal may be to emphasize quality assurance to get the post-quantum cryptographic migrations right the first time and to execute subsequent migrations through sprints (e.g., initiatives). A design goal is to make migrations lean, predictable, and repeatable. Without attention to quality assurance, some organizations face a severe technical risk that the hybrid cryptographic environment may not be as cryptographically agile as needed resulting in costly redesign delays.

Quality Truism

It is better to prevent quality defects than to fix them.
—Paul Le Dressay (1976)

Quality assurance occurs before doing work like post-quantum cryptographic migrations. Quality assurance includes following lean migration processes (e.g., testing and release management), and using templates (e.g., post-quantum cryptographic migration sprint plans) and checklists (post-quantum cryptographic migration validation checklist). These can be developed and refined in the proof-of-concept phase for post-quantum cryptographic migration use cases or during project and service management optimization sprints to develop checklists. These quality assurance artifacts, aligned with ITIL service management, can

Migrate

Initiate	Migration Strategy and Plan	Migration Design	Migration Configuration	Migration Proof of Concept	Migrate	Validate

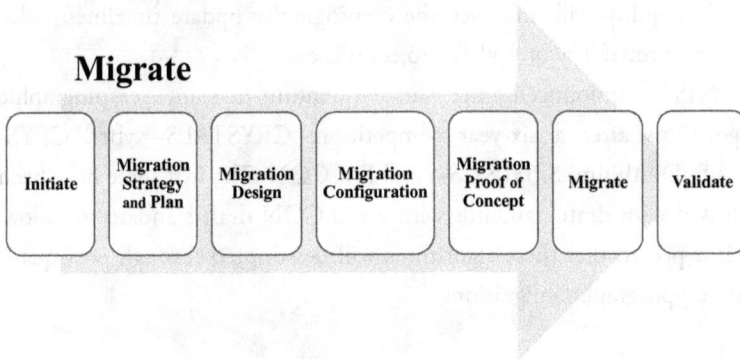

Figure 4.4 Post-quantum cryptographic migration project delivery

be used in subsequent post-quantum cryptographic migration sprints, projects, and initiatives.

Proof-of-Concept and Quality Assurance

Earlier we introduced an output of the cryptographic inventory analysis is to identify post-quantum cryptographic migration use cases to simplify the migration process (Canadian Forum for Digital Infrastructure Resilience 2023, 32). Use cases act like quality assurance templates that allow a quick start on most migration work. Each use case can benefit from a proof-of-concept/quality control phase prior to migration sprints into the production environment (Figure 4.4). The proof-of-concept phase is both a quality management and an upskilling opportunity for potentially complex migrations ahead: "The new algorithms are not, by and large, a drop-in replacement. They have limitations relative to the algorithms they are replacing and need careful fine-tuning and engineering to fit into existing systems" (Pupillo et al. 2023, 32). The technical team experiments with the post-quantum cryptographic migration configuration, process, and sequence to arrive at a lean and low-risk approach akin to project critical path scheduling.

Once user acceptance testing is completed, the proof-of-concept phase is finished, training is completed, and migration checklists and processes have been developed, the migration is executed. After migrating the post-quantum cryptography, the team member completes a validation (quality control check to find and fix defects) to determine whether the migration was successful. Caution is advised as the proof-of-concept version may linger in the production environment waiting for wide-scale rollout. Therefore, seek a sustained collaboration with the technical teams to keep the transition to post-quantum cryptography moving and the technical teams learning.

Migration planners are advised against hasty migrations as they can introduce vulnerabilities:

> It is essential to understand that a hasty migration to post-quantum security systems can introduce new vulnerabilities which could be exploited using conventional hacking methods. These vulnerabilities might arise from oversights, design flaws, or implementation errors. There could also be issues related to interoperability and backward compatibility, complicating the transition (Mosca and Piani 2023, 9).

Beyond the scope of this program management book are the IT operational and technical activities regarding post-quantum cryptography cutover and the disposal of any legacy technologies. Team morale is positively impacted when the proof-of-concept migration is proven successful, and the organization has demonstrated a way to progress toward post-quantum cryptographic security.

Quality Assurance Guides

A critical success factor for successful migrations is quality assurance including quality management processes, templates, and checklists. These can be developed and used for use case migrations to improve quality and reduce risk. Therefore, the project manager will build these activities into the project plan.[‡] The migration process, templates, and checklists may require tailoring for each type of migration (e.g., the public certificate authority/public key infrastructure cutover process will

---

[‡] In *Cybersecurity Training*, we detail how to plan, develop, and pilot test processes, templates, checklists, and training materials within a hybrid project delivery approach.

Migrate

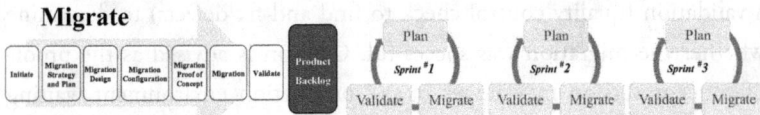

Figure 4.5 Migration proof-of-concept project and migration initiatives

differ from a database encryption cutover process or SSH connections cutover process).

Post-Quantum Cryptographic Migration Strategy

One of the final decisions prior to implementing post-quantum cryptographic migrations is to develop and approve the migration strategy into the new cryptographic environment. The migration strategy will likely start with a few ideas at the start of the awareness process and then be elaborated over time until it is a formal document aligned with ITIL strategy management best practices. For example, the senior technical team can establish the migration approach, develop quality assurance and control supports, and provide training for less experienced team members to execute each migration step through a sprint approach (Figure 4.5). A key benefit of this approach is that it frees up highly experienced cybersecurity leadership for other tasks while more junior team members execute the cryptographic use case migration sprints, supported with lean processes, training, and checklists.

Should team members encounter migration issues, the more experienced cybersecurity colleagues can assist. Leaderboards can be used to track and celebrate migration success. Leaderboards can improve cybersecurity SME engagement thereby reducing migration errors and improving efficiency.

The IT and cybersecurity leadership carefully consider the migration sequence as there are many migration options. For example, the cryptographic migration strategy may be to prioritize *easy* migrations while the team is still learning. The first *easy* migrations may also be used to fine-tune processes, templates, and checklists and to develop migration skills. Some refer to these easy migrations as the "low hanging fruit" approach (Cloud Security Alliance 2021, 30) and are often ideally suited to proof-of-concept migration sprints. For example, the technical team may choose to migrate to new key exchange algorithms first (because only the key length needs to be increased, Pupillo et al. 2023, 32). Indeed, attackers often look for known *low-hanging fruit vulnerabilities* that afford an easier attack vector. Another strategy is to first migrate the most critical data sets as identified in the cryptographic inventory (e.g., the organization's *crown jewels*). The technical leadership is responsible for the migration strategy that fits their unique organization and capabilities.

The post-quantum cryptographic migration use cases (e.g., *crown jewels* or *low-hanging fruit*) are first validated with the hybrid project management approach then subsequent migrations can be completed through sprints (Figure 4.5). Post-quantum cryptographic projects will be a significant undertaking for most organizations, and a program management approach can reduce risks and deliver the intended level of quality.

The reader is cautioned that "it is challenging to securely implement [post-quantum cryptographic] schemes even for cryptographic experts" (CSIRO 2021, 10). Therefore, the migration order is considered such as migrating the most critical assets early after the migration process has been tested, validated, and optimized (e.g., proof-of-concept).

Quantum Enabling Projects

When taking a holistic approach to cybersecurity readiness (people, process, and technology), there are projects and initiatives that enable quantum technologies adoption toward post-quantum cryptography, cryptographic agility, and other quantum-related projects. These projects and initiatives do not neatly fit into the previously described quantum program of projects (e.g., speaking at universities about quantum technology internships), we include a catch-all category of *quantum-enabling* projects. As the complete scope of quantum-enabling projects can be broad they are not reflected in our program Gantt chart (Figure 4.2) but are included here because there may be other projects outside the quantum program of projects and initiatives that can contribute to quantum program success.

Quantum Program Management Conclusion

The multitude of projects in the quantum program is diverse and varies from technical (e.g., post-quantum cryptographic migrations) to nontechnical (e.g., initiating quantum awareness projects). Project diversity, criticality, and urgency can be managed by adopting, tailoring, and combining standards and frameworks and applying the *Goldilocks Principle* to get the right amount. While there is an ITIL Portfolio Management practice, we align, tailor, and combine the standards from the Project Management Institute for project, program, and agile project management as they are applicable to most projects, most of the time. Aligning with best practices reduces quantum program risks and increases the likelihood the right level of quality is delivered (e.g., value).

These quantum projects and initiatives are driven by business, IT, and cybersecurity strategies. Quantum use cases are prioritized and managed by a PMO using the product backlog concept. The quantum business use cases (e.g., aviation engineering optimization) may be prioritized outside of the IT department with a business steering committee while project selection and prioritization of quantum technology projects, including post-quantum cryptographic migrations are likely to be planned and prioritized by IT leadership.

CHAPTER 5

Quantum Project Management

> *Migrating from conventional cryptography toward post-quantum cryptography will be a very time- and resource-consuming task. Judging from previous migrations this process might well take over five years* (TNO 2023, 3).

Given the complexity, criticality, and duration of the program of quantum projects and initiatives, in this book, our value proposition is to align with best practices found in global standards and frameworks and follow a program and hybrid project management approach to improve the probability of successful quantum projects and initiatives.

Hybrid Project Management for Quantum Transition Projects

The hybrid project management approach (Figure 2.8) is applicable to most digital transformation projects, including quantum projects, since it follows generally accepted practice: initiate, plan, design, build, test (quality control), transition to production (T2P), go-live and stabilize, concluding with project close out. There are adaptive iterations where necessary (e.g., problem solving in the design phase). The hybrid project delivery approach is tailored for the specific project, and external best practices may be combined (e.g., ITIL's Service Validation and Testing practice is used during testing).

Initiate

Projects are initiated according to the program schedule that reflects the timing of quantum strategic projects. The hybrid project delivery approach is used to implement most quantum use cases (the *demand* in ITIL's Service Value System, Figure 2.1). A key objective in the initiation phase is to create a project charter that reflects the quantum use case. A project charter template (e.g., one-page infographic) quickly guides the user (e.g., project manager) to complete a project charter. The organization's PMO may already have a charter template and if not, developing a project charter template could be added to the project management optimization projects and sprints. Developing templates to support quantum projects is an example of a project management optimization initiative. The project manager and sponsor (e.g., ITIL's service owner) collaborate on the project charter and provide it to leadership for permission to proceed to the planning phase. For longer projects, and for projects with multiple teams joining at different phases, it is best practice to create a project charter that can be reused throughout the project to orient new team members as they onboard. Therefore, templates can guide the project manager to develop project charters that are useful throughout the project.

In this quantum program of projects, the program manager, technical leadership, and sponsors will prioritize and sequence projects and initiatives. There will be some projects that implement a product (e.g., server) or service (e.g., training), and when completed, the team moves to the next project(s) according to the schedule. However, there are projects that once completed, continual improvement or migration sprints are implemented and managed through the product backlog (Figures 4.5 and 5.1).

The sprints might be heterogeneous where the migration sprints (Figure 5.1A) are interlaced with sprints to implement technologies (Figure 5.1B), improve processes (Figure 5.1C), or upskill people (Figure 5.1D) to use the new technologies.

There are at least four types of quantum cybersecurity continual improvement projects and initiatives (sprints) that can be widely applied to most quantum projects:

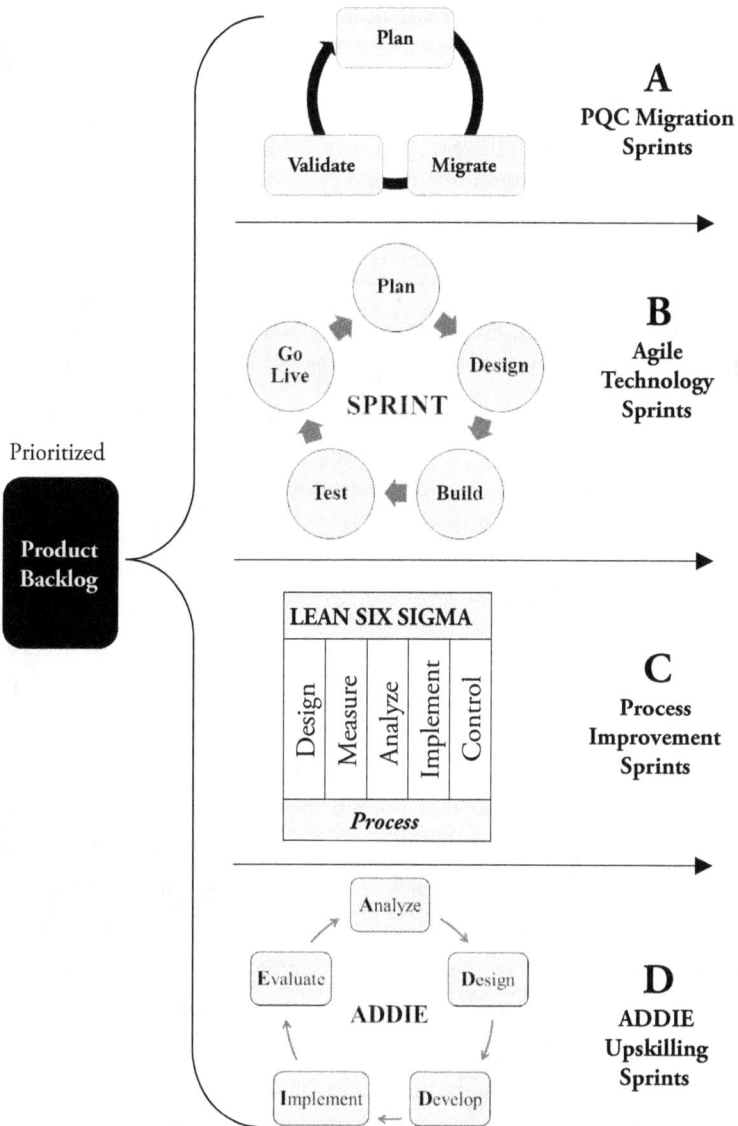

Figure 5.1 Prioritized product backlog sprints

1. Post-quantum cryptography migration sprints that go through the plan, migrate, and validate phases guided by training, lean processes, and checklists,

2. Technology sprints where software, hardware, devices, integration, updates, and configuration optimizations are implemented to support the quantum use cases,

3. Process optimization sprints to develop lean processes to support the quantum program of projects, initiatives, and services,

4. Upskilling sprints to develop competence (knowledge, skills, and experience) in quantum technologies.

These sprints may be combined as a holistic project. For example, the organization may implement post-quantum cryptography through consecutive sprints (Figure 5.2A) but may first have to upgrade technologies to receive the new cryptography (Figure 5.2B). Training may follow new technologies sprints, then cryptographic migrations (Figure 5.2C). Similarly, processes may need to be improved, and technology implemented before the migrations can begin (Figure 5.2D) followed by a stream of post-quantum cryptographic migrations (Figure 5.2A). Therefore, the prioritization and sequence of projects are determined by the IT and security architects and managed through the prioritized product backlog.

Therefore, most quantum projects can be delivered with either hybrid project management or through continual improvement sprints (e.g., initiatives). When complexity, duration, and impact increase, using the hybrid project management delivery approach brings greater formality and improves the probability of project success (Figure 2.8). Smaller projects (e.g., initiatives) that are more routine and less complex and time-consuming can be managed through the product backlog (Figure 5.1).

Projects and continual improvement initiatives are managed through program management governance and is outlined in PMI's *Standard for Program Management* with greater detail than ITIL's abbreviated project and portfolios practices. Given the criticality and complexity of the quantum program of projects, tailoring, and combing the fundamentals of program management is an ideal early optimization project with attention to governance and reporting. Once projects are initiated and a project charter is approved, the project progresses through a governance stage gate (control gate) and the planning phase begins.

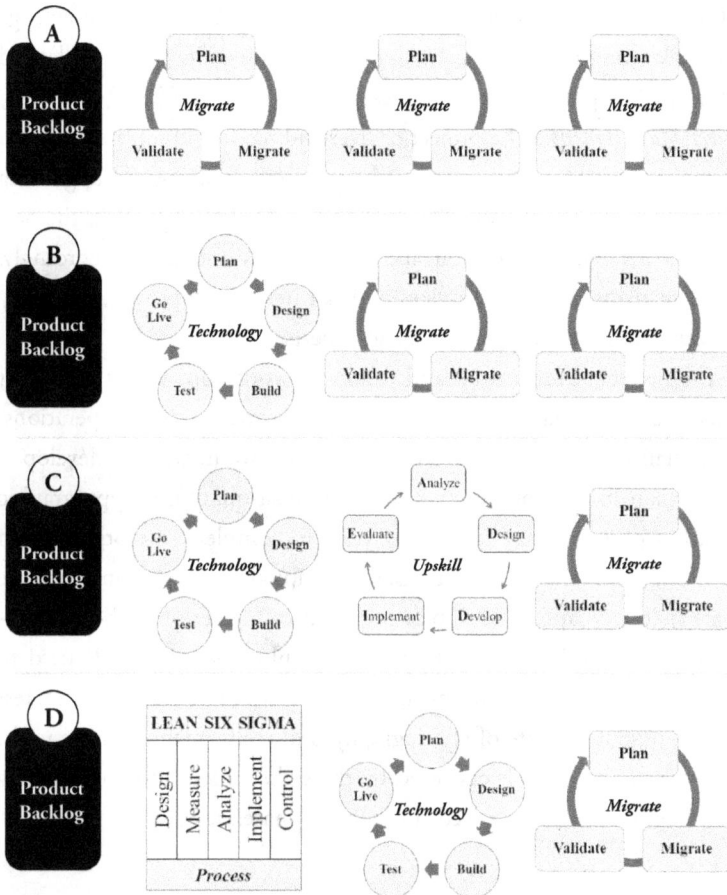

Figure 5.2 Quantum continual improvement

Plan

> *Rushing the process of migration to postquantum cryptography might itself create security issues which could be exploited even by attackers who use only traditional methods.* (Mosca and Piani 2023, 9).

The project charter is an input to the project plan phase (Figure 2.8). The purpose of the plan phase is to create a minimum viable project plan detailing the project objectives regarding scope, budget, schedule, risk, quality, resources, communications, stakeholders, procurement, and integration management (e.g., the PMBOK® Guide knowledge areas). Planning quantum technology projects benefits from a balanced and formal approach (e.g., as presented in *Shields Up: Cybersecurity Project Management*). The project charter and scope will set the direction for the project. For example, is the project replacing or upgrading technology? The IT and security architects and others will select the best strategies for the organization and stakeholders and plan accordingly. The team plans quantum services with an iterative approach, gradually including additional stakeholders and experts.

The project team sets up and facilitates workshops with the project sponsor, subject matter experts from the business side of operations, IT specialists, and perhaps outside vendors to iteratively develop a project plan for the quantum project. As post-quantum cryptographic migration program may take many years to complete, the organization will do well to account for a sustained capital and operating expense program (e.g., CapEx and OpEx implications). There may be preparatory work to fund like procuring cryptography discovery tools used to create an inventory, quantum-capable penetration testing tools to test the post-migration state of cryptography, and conformance testing tools. Once the project plan is endorsed by the stakeholders and approved by leadership, the project proceeds to the next phase: design.

Design

With an approved project plan, the team can begin the design phase (Figure 2.8) using the same workshop approach successfully used in the planning phase. Reusing project approaches and artifacts like templates and processes reduces risk and improves quality. The goal of the design phase is to elaborate the preliminary design outlined in the business case that was funded and approved. The design phase benefits from thinking through the steps to create the design (e.g., a post-quantum cryptographic migration differs from a quantum technologies implementation). Where possible, follow mature cybersecurity practices like *secure by design*. While we align with design principles in NIST special publications (e.g., "Minimum Security Requirements for Federal Information and Information Systems" or the "Security and Privacy

Controls for Information Systems and Organizations") other standards like ISO/IEC 27000 Information Security series can guide the organization to elicit, document, and approve quantum requirements. Regardless of the preferred cybersecurity standard or framework, the program management approach in this book can be applied with tailoring to the reader's unique organization.

During the design phase, subject matter experts (technical and nontechnical) collaborate and bring their unique perspectives and requirements: the project manager brings project management processes, tools, and methods, and IT security represents cybersecurity standards (e.g., ISO/IEC 31001) or frameworks (e.g., NIST Cybersecurity Framework). Business users bring other security requirements to be *designed-in* like those from the Health Insurance Portability and Accountability Act for healthcare, Payment Card Industry Data Security Standard for banking, and Space Data Association Cybersecurity Best Practices for safe and secure satellite communications. The design workshop follows a lean agenda that allows the stakeholders to develop a fit-for-purpose design that can get approved and add value.

Quantum Cybersecurity Workshop Agenda

The quantum cybersecurity workshop agenda drives workshop activity to create a successful design. The project manager or workshop facilitator works with subject matter experts to develop the agenda. The technical team may use some of the 29 common cryptographic use cases and protocols outlined by the Canadian Forum for Digital Infrastructure Resilience (2023, 32) teams. For example, a cryptographic migration agenda may include:

1. Workshop overview and purpose,
2. General migration strategies and tactics,
   a. Migrate primitives (e.g., symmetric and asymmetric cryptography, hash, MACs),

b. Migrate protocols (e.g., Kerberos, TLS, FTPS, mTLS, LDAPS),

c. Tabletop migration exercises to identify and elaborate the practical considerations and risk analysis for each type of end-to-end migration and cutover (e.g., interoperability risks and issues) and to find the optimal chain of cryptographic migration,

d. Prioritize the migrations and sequence (e.g., crown jewels after proof-of-concept migrations),

3. Migration schedule, resources, and budget,

4. Project risks and issues,

5. Next steps.

The workshop agenda guides the team to develop the design using a design document template from the PMO or generated online. Cryptographic agility is also *designed-in*. We leave it to the reader to learn about workshop facilitation best practices and instead, we focus on the project management side of workshops.

Quantum Design Document

The goal of the design phase is to create a minimum viable design according to stakeholders' requirements; the design document has just enough detail to guide the build phase (e.g., the *Goldilocks Principle*). The design template is aligned with ITIL practices (e.g., has sufficient detail for configuration management requirements) and is tailored for the organization's projects. Therefore, include the IT and security architects, service management specialists (e.g., release manager), and others when developing templates to ensure project and service management alignment and integration. As the type of project varies, so does the content of the design document and template; for example, a cryptographic migration design document will be different than a design document to configure a quantum software application and supporting hardware. The PMO can prioritize template development to support the program of quantum projects.

Design Workshops: Quantum Technologies

Organizations are beginning to implement quantum technologies developed for specific purposes (e.g., optimization rather than simulation problems). Quantum technologies support either business use cases (e.g., manufacturing optimization) and/or quantum cybersecurity applications like quantum random number generators. Quantum technology design templates and artifacts may be based on classical computing design documents such as (i) application detailed design, (ii) low-level hardware design, and (iii) integration design documents. A fundamental requirement in these technology design documents is to design-in cryptographic agility; indeed, the quantum technologies design template may include a section for cryptographic agility requirements as detailed in the organization's security and cryptography policies. Another section to add is to detail any regulatory or accreditation requirements related to the technology being designed. A key point is subject matter experts create and endorse the design document, and it is approved by leadership representing the end users and IT leadership. Again, there are many design-related resources if one approaches implementing quantum technologies (e.g., hardware, software, and integration) as a digital transformation design activity.

Design Workshops: Foundation Projects

Successful post-quantum cryptographic migrations and technology projects in general are dependent upon the degree of project and technology service management maturity. Therefore, quantum champions are advised to review project and service management best practices and tune them for the upcoming decade of projects and cryptographic migrations. They may also review standards like the Organizational Project Management Maturity Model from the Project Management Institute or the ITIL Framework for optimization inspiration. For those outside the ITIL Framework, the COBIT technology management approach includes a technology maturity model to guide teams to develop lean approaches, especially for the many post-quantum cryptographic migration projects including cutover and technology disposal. For example, a Lean Six Sigma approach can identify process *pain points* and guide improvements to reduce post-quantum cryptographic migration risks. Templates and FAQs can be developed to support frequently used processes (see Figure 2.13 for the ADDIE model to develop templates, checklists, and other guides). The ADDIE model can also be used to develop quantum-related training that was detailed in *Cybersecurity Training: A Pathway to Readiness*. Project and technology service management foundation projects can provide training, tools, and processes for the many quantum projects to follow.

Design Workshops: Cybersecurity

Some of the early cybersecurity projects for most organizations will be to ensure a minimum viable cybersecurity foundation is provided to protect against steal now, decrypt later risks. These projects may be diverse, ranging from people upskilling, to process improvement, to technology optimization projects to address any cybersecurity risks. The technology subject matter experts can refer to best practices like Australia's *Essential Eight* (e.g., multifactor authentication and regular patching) or CISA's *Cybersecurity Performance Goals* to identify and prioritize the target requirements and projects and initiatives to achieve, maintain, and improve the organization's minimum viable cybersecurity foundation.

The cybersecurity design workshop may have a standing crypto-graphic agility checkpoint to maintain quality. For example, when the cybersecurity team designs security, they refer to the organization's "centrally provided set of cryptographic libraries and services that abstract algorithms in use from application and infrastructure teams; and identify data field and size dependencies, and adjust surrounding databases, datastores, protocols and other software that assumes current fixed field sizes" (Joseph 2022, 241). Some data and systems may benefit from both classical and quantum cryptographic protection to resist quantum attacks (Mosca and Piani 2022, 4) and be engineered in the design phase. The IT and security architects will lead the design process while the project manager supports with project management tools, processes, templates, and checklists (e.g., document the risks in a risk register while the subject matter experts discuss *challenges* or *threats*).

Design Workshops: Post-Quantum Cryptographic Migration

Post-quantum cryptographic migration design workshops follow the traditional workshop approach by detailing the workshop scope, objectives, goals, agenda, rules, and so forth. The cryptographic subject matter experts analyze the different cryptographic requirements and choose a post-quantum cryptographic scheme to implement (e.g., cryptography use cases, Canadian Forum for Digital Infrastructure Resilience 2023, 32). Technical teams detail the target cryptographic environment (e.g., hybrid cryptography) in the design documents. During the test phase, the cybersecurity team will determine if their algorithm selection and configuration are viable (e.g., proof-of-concept). Indeed, during testing, they may discover *defects* like excessive memory usage and may look to another cryptographic solution (e.g., problem-solving iterations, Figure 2.8) or upgrade the memory in this example. Some devices require multiple or heterogeneous cryptography which makes migrating to post-quantum cryptography complex (e.g., enhanced interoperability risks especially with hybrid keys).

A key goal of the migration workshops is to understand the dependency chain of migration where the team determines and prioritizes the order of post-quantum cryptographic migrations (e.g., use cases, hardware, applications). They may map out the post-quantum cryptographic migration use case scenarios and conduct a risk analysis to find the best migration sequence and cutover. The project manager may facilitate a tabletop, multiyear migration exercise to better understand dependencies, sequencing, budgeting, risks, and other variables for a successful program of projects and smooth operational transition.

An early design decision will be how to implement post-quantum cryptographic resistant treatments, for example, what will comprise the hybrid cryptographic environment (e.g., use a quantum random number generator with classical cryptography)? Will the strategy be a phased approach or a direct cutover to post-quantum cryptography? The IT and security architects will determine an operational strategy of backward compatibility and interoperability between classical, hybrid, and post-quantum cryptography. Again, the IT and security architects will take their time to plan out the implementation, and perhaps to *game out* the different implementation options. The overall project plan will account for a comprehensive and detailed analysis to get the right migration design.

Once the technical teams *endorse* the design, it is given to leadership for *approval*. Once approval to proceed is given, the stage gate to the build phase opens, and building and configuring begins. The quantum program of projects and initiatives is a multiyear undertaking and formal change control reduces risk and improves governance.

To conclude, by understanding the scope and complexity of the design (e.g., determining the dependency chain of migration and conducting an end-to-end risk analysis of the cryptographic migration), the project team can create better duration and cost estimates. An improved understanding leads to predictable and repeatable quantum projects including post-quantum cryptographic migrations. Design workshops are iterative collaborations where the outputs, for example, are used to develop a feasible design document that can be approved. Again, the *Goldilocks Principle* applies, not too much nor too little content in the design document, but just enough to get approval and guide the build teams.

Build

The build team(s) follow the approved design and commence building and configuring (Figure 2.8). The technical specialists like intelligent automation engineers, cryptographic analysts, hardware implementers, and instructional designers build, configure, and develop the product or service the project produces (e.g., project deliverables). The project team monitors their progress and keeps in regular contact at weekly risks and issues meeting or at stand-up meetings. The builders may create an *as built* document and will update the configuration *source of truth* records such as in the configuration register or service management catalog. It is prudent to include configuration records updates as a build phase exit requirement since *as built* details may be of great importance to future colleagues.

Test

It is widely recommended that organizations begin *experimenting* with quantum technologies, quantum use case development and programming, and post-quantum cryptography algorithms; we encourage experimenting but distinguish it from testing. We align with project and service management and use the term *test* to determine if the technology under review is fit for purpose and provides the expected value (detailed in the project design documents). Experimenting is quantum champions learning about the capabilities of quantum technologies and applying them to organizational problems and opportunities in a *laboratory setting* (e.g., in an environment separated from the production environment and sometimes known as a *playpen*). In this book, testing is a quality control activity and phase—find and fix defects—to ensure the product or service being produced by the project is fit for purpose. Experimentation may lead to the development of a quantum application that will be tested prior to its release into the production environment.

The project manager and technical team (e.g., quality or test manager) to develop a high-level test strategy and lower-level plan that ranges from outlining the overall testing approach, key risks, responsibilities, test deliverables, etc. More detailed planning may consider the test environment, test data, testing tools, types of tests (in scope and out of scope), test scripts, etc. We combine and tailor ITIL's Service Validation and Testing practice within our hybrid project delivery approach (Figures 2.2 and 2.8). The key testing processes can be followed and tailored for classical and quantum technologies and include:

Develop the test strategy: Describe the overall approach based on criticality and goals of testing. Include roles and responsibilities, any relevant policies and procedures, high-level schedules and milestones, key risks and issues, resources, quality management, metrics, and reporting.

Develop the test plan: Describe in more detail the plan, test scope, schedule, and activities; detailed test cases; data and environment; resources; defect management; entry and exit criteria; metrics and reporting; and test automation. The testing team may plan to test the dependency chain of post-quantum cryptographic migration including interoperability and backward compatibility. The user acceptance process for the quantum-related service can also be planned and managed for risks. The goal is to develop a lean plan with just enough detail to guide the testing teams to find and fix defects.

Verify the test strategy and plan: Once the test strategy and plan are developed, they are validated for completeness and approved by testing leadership and the project sponsor.

Prepare the test environment: Prepare and establish a baseline of the test environment for the testing. Throughout the testing process, automation may be used, especially to return the test environment to the baseline if it will be used many times. Some testers use testing and test environment management software.

Test: Follow the test plan for the new quantum service (e.g., post-quantum cryptographic migration) with manual and/or automated testing techniques and procedures. A common risk is iterative problem solving can extend testing activities resulting in delays. The testing team documents test results in a test register.

Evaluate test results and report: Test results are compared with expected results (e.g., validate the cryptographic migration), and any gaps are addressed (e.g., identify gaps, workarounds, next steps, and outstanding actions).

Test close out: The team returns the test environments to their baseline environment (e.g., default configuration) after testing. There may be lessons learned resulting in the opportunity to update testing processes, training materials, templates, and checklists leading to improved testing and go-live execution.

Not only is testing designed to determine whether the technological solution works as per the approved design, but the technical team also evaluates performance (e.g., processing time and memory usage), usability, security, and other performance elements. The testing team may face the *Goldilocks Challenge*: balance performance, security, and usability. See Perryman et al. (2024, 30) for more about the performance—security trade-off.

Organizations are advised to heed the advice to diligently test post-quantum cryptographic solutions: "Regardless, all organizations must test quantum migrations before implementing at full-scale in production environments. Catastrophic operational interruption can result from inadequate testing" (Cloud Security Alliance 2021, 34). Indeed, it is prudent to inform stakeholders early in the project that without their assistance in critical phases like testing, the project can fail! Quantum champions may use language like a *catastrophic operational interruption* with a detailed account of the effects on the organization to convey the appropriate level of criticality.

While the organization experiments and tests quantum technologies (e.g., evaluate technology security), the organization will also test and evaluate enterprise and third-party security. Enterprise security involves protecting the organization's people and its business against quantum risks. Third-party security is also added to the testing agenda to protect the organization against quantum risks that originate from vendors, partners, customers, and other stakeholders. Thus, the scope and complexity of testing go beyond evaluating quantum technologies.

Testing may also be a proof-of-concept exercise where the feasibility of future technology implementations or migrations are evaluated including cryptographic agility requirements. In addition to determining feasibility, the technical team identifies the *best* way; for example, the best way to migrate cryptographic primitives (e.g., symmetric and asymmetric cryptography, hash, MACs) and minimize risks and effort, and achieve quality targets. Once the *best* way is developed in the proof-of-concept phase, migrations can become lean and with support (e.g., templates, checklists, procedures, and training). These supports are also pilot tested for usability and other test criteria. The result of the proof-of-concept phase is that the feasibility of the technology is determined, supports are developed, and training is provided to reduce implementation and cryptographic migration risks, and to achieve the desired quality outcomes.

Thus, the test phase is a critical phase and in *Quantum Cybersecurity*, we align with best practices, and match project criticality and complexity with the degree of test formality and comprehensiveness. For example, a project manager may conduct more testing for implanted cardiac device technology and less for a new printer; testing quantum technologies may be approached with the same guidance. Some organizations include a stage gate where testing approval is required to move to the final pre-go-live phase: the T2P phase.

Transition to Production

The transition to production (T2P) phase (Figure 2.8) involves the final activities to move the quantum product or service from the test to the production environment where it can be used by the end user. Organizations can combine and tailor ITIL's Release and Deployment Management practice to develop T2P processes, templates, and checklists.

Moving from the test to the production environment is risky as the new digital product or service may disrupt business operations in the live environment; however, with thorough testing and careful planning with the release manager, the team can use T2P checklists to reduce risks related to technology release and deployment. For example, the security team can follow a T2P checklist to harden the new quantum service by eliminating old ciphers and libraries and identify roll-back triggers and metrics should the migration fail. Templates, checklists, and other quality management aids can be developed as part of the project management continual improvement initiatives, evaluated during the proof-of-concept phase, and used in subsequent projects and sprints. When T2P activities are complete, the new quantum service is ready to transition to the production environment for its intended use. In *Shields Up*, we detail how to work with the *Change Authorization Board* to manage the T2P phase to achieve a smooth and predictable transition to the production environment.

Go-Live

> *If we wait for everything to be perfect, we will never go live.*
> —Dr. Marc Harrison, Former CEO, Cleveland Clinic Abu
> Dhabi

The quantum service is released into the production environment and monitored for stability, performance, and effectiveness. Project teams often stabilize the service while collaborating vendors are still on the project. Organizations can use ITIL's Service Desk and Incident Management practices to monitor KPIs related to new quantum technology adoption. Quantum technologies end users are encouraged to raise a ticket with the service desk if they encounter any incidents; tracking incidents improves the organization's understanding of the new technology adoption. For example, the incident queue manager categorizes incidents related to a *break-fix* technical problem, or a lack of understanding (e.g., insufficient learning). By accurately categorizing the incident, the correct resolver group is assigned to resolve the incident.

While some project team members are monitoring and perhaps stabilizing the new quantum service in the production, others are completing project close out activities.

Close Out

The final project phase is close out (Figure 2.8). When the new quantum service has been released, monitored, and stabilized, if necessary, it will be time to close out the project. Project managers can use a project close out template to develop the close out report and use a close out checklist to guide completing the final project activities. The close out report may have an appendix related to any cryptographic inventory details and assurance the configuration management records are updated (e.g., include configuration updates as a close out requirement to aid future cryptography management). The close out report may list unmet requirements and new quantum optimization requests. These can be managed with the product backlog in the continual improvement process (Figures 2.10 and 5.1). Post-quantum cryptographic migrations will include updating the cryptographic inventory and a lessons learned exercise, especially if the wisdom gained can be immediately applied to the next project, initiative, or migration.

To conclude, there are many quantum projects ranging from nontechnical to technical, resulting in some variability of the project management delivery approach (e.g., pilot testing quantum awareness materials is different from testing new technologies; however, both are quality control activities during the test phase). Standard project delivery approaches (e.g., hybrid and agile) can be used for quantum projects with guidance from best practices found in standards (e.g., project and program management standards) and frameworks (e.g., service management frameworks). A critical success factor is to apply just the right amount of program, project, and service management—the *Goldilocks Principle*. Seasoned project managers will understand that once the project plan is approved, the real work begins, and governance is another critical success factor seasoned project participants value.

Quantum Program Governance

> *Quantum computing will enable great innovations in the future but will be accompanied by great risk* (World Economic Forum 2022b, 8).

While the program of quantum projects and initiatives is underway, governance is a critical success factor. As criticality, risk, and project complexity increase, it is best practice to increase governance; therefore, we align with governance detailed in the ITIL Framework and in project and program management standards. Governance begins with planning. The quantum program sponsors will plan and execute governance activities to (i) monitor, (ii) evaluate, and (iii) direct the quantum program of projects. The project manager can build in reporting that supports these three governance activities and invites the program sponsor to a program communications requirements and design meeting. For example, the project manager asks the quantum program sponsor "what information about the quantum program of projects do you require?" Project managers can apply best practices from project and program communications management to provide valued reports. In *Shields Up*, we detail cybersecurity project communications (including reporting and status meeting strategies).

Project Risk Management

Fundamentally, cybersecurity is about risk management. The NIST Cybersecurity Framework's functions reflect risk management: govern, identify, protect, detect, respond, and recover. Project management is also about risk management: the only reason why projects fail is risks become issues that are not sufficiently resolved resulting in delays, cost over-runs, quality gaps, and other indicators of a failed project. Therefore, risk management, including enterprise risk management (NIST 2022b), underlies our hybrid project and program management approaches. The main reason why status reports are desired is that all programs, projects, and initiatives face risks and issues and in the case of quantum cybersecurity risks, with potentially catastrophic effects. If the project was risk-free or with only low severity risks and low-impact issues, then projects are likely on track, and detailed reports are not required! Therefore, program and project status reports involve a great deal of risk management reporting,[*] along with schedule and budget information.

Status Reporting

The good thing about risk management and reporting is that the basics found in standards and frameworks are generally accepted, applicable to most projects, are easy to use, and are effective. Status reports

---

[*] Recall that there are many code words used for risks and issues such as *challenges* and *difficulties* that may also be used in status reports adding to the amount of risk content.

Collaborate and plan
communications based
on stakeholder needs

Meet stakeholder
communications needs
and adjust if necessary

Plan

Quantum Project
Communications

Manage

Quantum Project
Communications

Monitor & Control

Quantum Project
Communications

Ensure timely and appropriate
collection, creation, distribution,
storage, retrieval, management,
monitoring, and the ultimate
disposition of project information

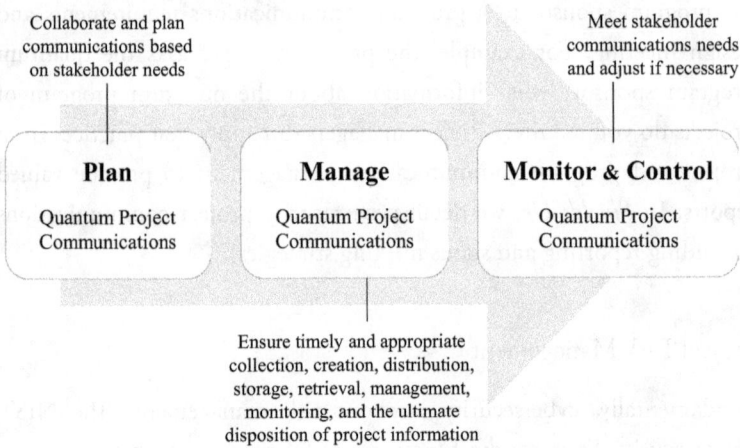

Figure 5.3 Quantum project communications management

may follow the project communications management process: plan, manage, monitor, and control communications (Figure 5.3). Therefore, we apply program and project risk and communications management best practices found in project management standards to guide status reporting. The project manager is in regular contact with the quantum program sponsors and stakeholders and can verify the right information is being provided—a continual improvement mindset.

Status reports can also include information about any gaps between planned and actual performance, and strategy attainment. The status report reader will want to understand what work is outstanding, and if the project is facing risks, what must be done to resolve the issues and get back on track. The reader wants to understand how close the project teams are to delivering the target solution or future state. Post-quantum cryptographic migration progress reports will include what has and has not been migrated in addition to standard reporting elements (e.g., top risks and issues, schedule KPIs). Status reporting is a regular occurrence, and developing and using communication templates reduces communication risks (e.g., incomplete information) and increases quality (e.g., the reader understands the next reporting period's actions and deliverables).

Program status reports differ slightly from program status reports since executives require different information from day-to-day reporting.

Instead, bring together key questions and requests for executive action. Avoid *watermelon* status reports and *never surprise your boss.*

Thus, governance is a process rather than an event; leadership establishes policies and procedures, identifies roles and responsibilities, and continuously monitors the status of projects and initiatives. Central to governance is monitoring and controlling risks and issues rather than performative status updates and avoiding bad news reports.

Service Management Operations

The project and initiative deliverables are used by end users to create value. After some period of use, end users may request configuration optimizations, new features, additional integration points, etc. These requests may be part of continual improvement.

Continual Improvement

The terms continuous and continual improvement are similar, but what is the difference? Continuous improvement involves ongoing enhancements that do not stop. Continual improvement goes further, where organizations look externally to benchmark, innovate, and improve. Therefore, in *Quantum Cybersecurity*, we use *continual improvement*, as featured in the ISO 9001 Quality Management standard, since it more closely aligns with the quality management goals and philosophy in this book.

There are many sources of requests for new or updated training, software applications, technologies, integration, and endpoint devices, or changes to business workflows, policies, and procedures. There may be requests to practice the response and recovery playbooks or for periodic quantum vulnerability testing. Security policies and procedures are regularly reviewed to determine if changes are required; updated policies and procedures often have knock-on effects, such as the need for training or technology enhancements. Organizations can group continual improvement requests into people, process, and technology categories to select the appropriate project or sprint delivery approach and team. These requests are prioritized and managed with the product backlog(s) as illustrated in Figure 2.10. Some of these requests may be complex requiring a full project delivery approach.

Quantum Projects

Major quantum projects are usually linked to achieving strategic objectives (e.g., cybersecurity readiness, Figures 2.14 and 4.2) and often follow the hybrid project management approach (Figure 2.8) with tailoring and combining. Organizations also continually improve through smaller projects called initiatives.

Quantum Initiatives

Smaller projects, known as initiatives,[†] are used to deliver and optimize training, technology, and processes (Figure 2.10). Initiatives require less governance (e.g., documentation and reporting) and fewer processes. IT departments may use a product backlog to prioritize technology optimization initiatives. A business operations steering committee may endorse and prioritize initiatives (and projects) in the product backlog. Notice continual improvement's ongoing, iterative, and adaptive nature aligns with best practices in ISO quality management, agile scrum, adaptive project management, ITIL service management, and other standards and frameworks, including cybersecurity.

To conclude this section, quantum project management is about applying best practices in the form of delivery approaches, processes, tools, and techniques. The hybrid project delivery approach is commonly used: initiate, plan, design, build, test, T2P, go-live, and close out. Iterations can be used to problem solve and to implement adaptive techniques (e.g., Lean Six Sigma).

Managing quantum initiatives also benefits from formal approaches like those from the Project Management Institute (e.g., Agile Practice Guide). We apply and tailor the hybrid project management approach

---

[†] Some use the term *initiatives* to mean major strategic or transformational projects. We apologize if we add confusion and use the term initiatives for smaller projects that do not require as much governance as larger projects.

(Figure 2.8) and combine it with best practices (Figures 2.14 and 3.9). Our value proposition is to judiciously apply, tailor and combine best practices found in standards and frameworks to reduce risks and achieve the right level of quality. Thus, the quantum program includes ongoing projects and initiatives (Figure 4.2).

Microlearning

When one broadly reads the literature, digital transformation due to AI and quantum technologies will continue for some time. The organizations' quest for continual improvement has resulted in a massive online body of knowledge to guide their efforts:

- For your industry, which is more common: continual or continuous improvement?
- What is a quality improvement quest? How does it work and how can it be applied to quantum projects?
- What continual improvement use cases in your industry and discipline?
- What are ISO 9001 continual improvement best practices and risks?

Conclusion

> UN Declares *2025 the International Year of Quantum Science and Technology*

Advances in quantum technologies research and development bring news each day of achievements and promises and have inspired the United Nations to declare 2025 as the International Year of Quantum Science and Technology. It is a call to grand action to explore and develop transformational change across industries and to protect against existential quantum cyberattacks. Critical business workflows may be optimized to provide innovative change and indeed market disruption. Quantum simulations can lead to breakthrough discoveries in materials science and medicine, for example. Forecasting for just about anything can be improved. However, quantum research and development are of little value unless they can be successfully implemented and adopted. To successfully implement quantum technologies, program and project management processes, generally accepted tools, and techniques are recommended.

We apply ITIL service management principles since project management is part of the end-to-end technology lifecycle beginning with the demand for quantum technologies through to project delivery, end-user adoption, optimization, and phase out of legacy technologies. A critical success factor for successful projects and technology management is to align with best practices and to tailor and combine standards (e.g., PMBOK® Guide and ISO 31000 Risk Management) and frameworks (ITIL Service Management Framework and the NIST Cybersecurity Framework). The perennial challenge is to find the "sweet spot" where just enough best practices are applied (e.g., the *Goldilocks Principle*).

There is scant literature and program management guidance to implement the range of quantum projects. We provide a program management approach to implementing quantum projects and initiatives. The organization begins and conducts a gap analysis to understand its current and future technological and cryptographic states. A discovery cryptographic inventory is used to understand current cryptography. The gap analysis results in a prioritized program of projects managed through the organization's project management office. The quantum projects (and initiatives) PMOs should be implementing include:

Minimum viable cybersecurity foundation projects: to protect against the steal now, decrypt later risks and is prioritized as one of the first projects,

Quantum awareness projects: to develop support, commitment, and enthusiasm for a decade or more of quantum projects and initiatives,

Project management optimization projects: to provide lean project and sprint delivery processes, templates, checklists, and training to plan, design, build, test, implement, and close out the many quantum-related projects and initiatives,

Service management optimization projects: to provide lean processes to procure, implement, support, and optimize the new quantum ecosystem,

Cryptographic agility projects: to provide the ability to quickly change cryptography and to avoid purchasing post-quantum cryptographically vulnerable technologies,

Post-quantum cryptographic migration projects: to migrate to NIST-endorsed cryptography to protect against post-quantum cryptographic attacks,

Quantum technologies: to support business use cases, the IT department will implement quantum technologies projects and initiatives (e.g., hardware and software) based on approved quantum business cases.

These projects can be tailored and managed with project and program management techniques and best practices and combined with standards and frameworks like the NIST Cybersecurity Framework and the ITIL Service Management Framework. We leave the next steps to the reader as you reread sections of this book and apply, tailor, and combine concepts to your quantum projects. We invite the reader to review *Shields Up:*

Cybersecurity Project Management for more about hybrid project management, including innovative risk management proven on implementing new and complex technologies and process improvement. *Cybersecurity Training: A Pathway to Readiness* guidance upskilling and associated learning guides, checklists, and templates. We invite the reader to connect with us on LinkedIn to participate in the extended practitioner community.

We wish you the best of luck on your quantum journey. We are excited for you since you are on an extraordinary journey as you will implement new innovations, discover new things, protect against existential threats, and do what project managers do best: initiate, plan, design, build, test, and deliver extraordinary value. It is a great time to be in quantum program management.

Sincerely and with thanks,
Greg and Ashkan

Glossary

Our glossary is tailored to quantum cybersecurity. Purists may find we may have tailored our definitions a bit too much. Still, we take some liberty to tailor and combine to create an applied glossary for *Quantum Cybersecurity* for the reader new to quantum technologies. The reader is encouraged to go online to find or generate additional information.

Agile project management: an iterative delivery approach to delivering requirements (see the companion Agile Manifesto).

Algorithm: a set of instructions (e.g., a suite of quantum circuits) to solve a problem or perform calculations.

Classical cryptography: cryptography that is secure against classical computing but not quantum computers (see also *post-quantum cryptography*).

COBIT: the Control Objectives for Information Technologies framework provides a governance and management framework to plan, implement, manage, and optimize digital products and services (see ITIL, an alternative framework).

Combine: bring together tools and processes from different standards and frameworks.

Computer security incident response team (CSIRT): comprises technical and nontechnical specialists who respond to and recover from cybersecurity incidents. They may follow an incident response and recovery playbook specific to their organization.

Cryptoanalysis: the study and analysis of cryptosystems for improvement purposes or to understand how to defeat cryptosystems (e.g., dual potentialities).

Cryptographic agility: the ability to update the organization's cryptography efficiently and effectively (e.g., update only the algorithms rather than replace devices).

Cryptographic bill of materials (CBOM): a standardized list of cryptographic components and libraries and their dependencies developed through a comprehensive discovery process of diverse systems, software, hardware, services, and infrastructure. Organizations use the CBOM to prioritize their migration to post-quantum cryptography.

Cryptographic diversity: applying multiple cryptographic solutions from multiple families of cryptography that are unlikely to be vulnerable to the same attack.

Cryptographic library: a suite of cryptographic algorithms used as tools for secure communications and data protection.

Cryptographically-relevant quantum computer: quantum technologies with sufficient capabilities to break public-key systems (e.g., asymmetric cryptography) used to protect systems with classical cryptography. Cryptographically relevant quantum computers are also known as cryptanalytically-relevant quantum computers. See Mosca's Z parameter that represents the arrival of a cryptographically-relevant quantum computer.

Cryptography: the study of ensuring the safe transfer and storage of information in an adversarial environment.

Cybersecurity: protecting the organization's information through risk management practices and processes (e.g., prevent, detect, and respond to cybersecurity incidents).

Cybersecurity readiness: the ability of organizations and people to predict and respond to cyber threats and opportunities. Organizations wishing to maintain and improve cybersecurity readiness include continual improvement practices like regular cybersecurity training. A minimum viable cybersecurity foundation that is continually improved is a prerequisite for cybersecurity readiness.

Cybersecurity resilience: the ability of the organization to respond and recover from cybersecurity incidents.

Demand: technology users request existing or new digital products or services, which is detailed in ITIL's Demand Management practice.

Discovery Tools: automated software that identifies where and how public-key cryptography is used in the digital ecosystem (e.g., hardware, software, operating systems, firmware, communication protocols, key platforms, and cryptographic libraries) including the cloud, data centers, and so on.

Dual potentialities of technology: technology is inherently neutral; however, it (quantum computing) can be used for good (cure diseases) or bad purposes (steal and decrypt).

Early adopters: individuals and organizations who use new technologies before others.

Encryption: the process of scrambling data so only the intended parties can unscramble it.

Encryptogeddon: a point in time when the collective negative impacts of threat actors using quantum technologies to break encryption with brute force techniques outweigh the benefits of quantum technologies.

Frameworks: best practices but usually exist in the absence of well-defined and globally accepted standards. Frameworks are less prescriptive and more flexible than standards.

Guide to the Project Management Body of Knowledge (PMBOK® Guide): the ANSI standard for project management representing best practices for most projects, most of the time.

Hybrid environment: a digital ecosystem where classical and quantum computing and algorithms co-exist (also known as a hybrid solution).

Initiative: a smaller project that requires less governance and supporting documentation. However, project management tools and processes (e.g., risk management) benefit initiatives (see also *project*).

ISO standards: guides embodying international best practices agreed upon by experts. They often have a certification pathway indicating meeting the required levels of quality to safely deliver the service or quality for which they are certified.

ITIL: the Information Technology Infrastructure Library is a service management framework of practices that outline how to plan, deliver, operate, and optimize digital services (see COBIT, an alternative framework).

Key establishment and management: set up and manage the cryptographic key process: generation, distribution, storage, access, and destruction.

Laggard adopters: individuals and organizations who use new technologies after others (e.g., after early adopters have stabilized the technology).

Minimum viable project and initiative: projects and initiatives to address technology or cybersecurity gaps. These projects represent achieving thresholds or foundations to build future innovations or leverage intended capabilities.

Mosca's Theorem: a mathematical equation to evaluate an organization's preparedness for the quantum era.

NIST Cybersecurity Framework: the American government National Institute of Standards and Technology (NIST) provides a cybersecurity approach of best practices to manage cybersecurity risks.

Noise: undesired interference with the quantum qubits during superposition resulting in errors. Quantum error correction in a fault-tolerant system mitigates noise to increase computational accuracy.

Noisy intermediate-scale quantum systems: quantum technologies that are too noisy (e.g., high computational error rates) to produce fault-tolerant computing.

No-regret project: a cost-effective project under a range of future risk scenarios where value is likely delivered.

Post-quantum cryptography: cryptographic algorithms that are presumed to be secure from both quantum and classical computer attacks (also known as quantum-safe cryptography and quantum-resistant cryptography; see also *classical cryptography*).

Project: a unique, temporary endeavor to produce a product or service requiring significant effort and governance to address risks and limited resources (see also *initiative*).

Public-key algorithms: the sender has a different key than the receiver (also known as asymmetric algorithms).

Public-key cryptography: a public key and private key algorithms are used to encrypt and decrypt data to prevent unauthorized access.

Public key infrastructure: the set of policies, procedures, software, and hardware required to create, manage, distribute, apply, store, and revoke digital certificates and public keys required for secure encryption.

Q2K: the challenge of preparing for a cryptographically-relevant quantum computer is compared to the challenges of preparing for Y2K (the year 2000 risk). However, Q2K differs as the risks are clearer but the date is uncertain.

Quantum advantage: a point in time where a quantum computer can solve a problem more efficiently and effectively (e.g., more accurately) than a classical computer.

Quantum business case: a high-level or strategic description of the quantum product or service, product, or service manager (e.g., service owner), contribution to strategy, benefits, timelines, costs, return on investment, and risks and issues.

Quantum business use case: a detailed or tactical description of how quantum technologies are applied to a specific business problem or opportunity. A quantum business use case can be part of the quantum business case (e.g., contribution to strategy).

Quantum cryptography: applying quantum properties to create cryptographic protocols like quantum key distribution (QKD).

Quantum cybersecurity readiness: a state of at least effective post-quantum cryptography and cryptographic agility enabled through continual improvement cycles (projects and initiatives) and built upon a minimum viable cybersecurity foundation.

Quantum error correction: techniques used to find and fix errors that occur in quantum calculations due to qubit fragility (e.g., noise and decoherence).

Quantum fault-tolerant: the entire design and implementation of quantum algorithms and processors to ensure accurate and reliable quantum calculations.

Quantum key distribution: QKD encrypts and decrypts data with the principles of quantum physics (e.g., superposition and entanglement); however, post-quantum cryptography is generally recommended over QKD.

Quantum readiness: the ability to manage risks related to quantum technologies in the categories of people, process, and technology including providing sufficient post-quantum cryptography, and developing and maintaining cryptographic agility. Quantum readiness assumes a minimum viable cybersecurity foundation is maintained and continually optimized for both quantum and classical technologies.

Quantum-safe cryptography: the study of cryptographic algorithms that are thought to be secure from both quantum and classical computer attacks (also known as post-quantum cryptography and quantum-resistant cryptography).

Quantum supremacy: a milestone when a quantum computer can perform tasks that would be impossible for a classical computer (also known as quantum primacy), regardless of the utility of the calculation.

Quantum technologies: technologies that apply the principles of quantum physics like quantum computers or quantum sensors.

Quantum vulnerable: a system susceptible to a quantum attack (e.g., the digital ecosystem may have insufficient post-quantum cryptography).

Qubit: the smallest unit of information in quantum computing, like a bit in classical computing, except a qubit can be in both states of 0 and 1 simultaneously (superposition property of quantum mechanics).

RSA cryptography: Rivest–Shamir–Adleman (1977) is a public-key encryption algorithm for secure data transmission to encrypt data using two different but linked keys.

SCADA system: Supervisory Control and Data Acquisition is an industrial (operational) control system used to control processes, manage real-time data, and interact with sensors, values, pumps, motors, and other devices. SCADA systems are widely used like in petrochemical industries, wastewater management systems, energy transportation, traffic lights, and other systems used in society.

SHA-2 migration: NIST determined the Secure Hash Algorithm (SHA)-1 should not be trusted and advised organizations to migrate to SHA-2.

Simulation: using quantum technologies to model and simulate physical and chemical systems at the quantum level.

Steal now, decrypt later: to steal data and wait until quantum tools are available to decrypt the data (also known as record now, exploit later).

Tailor: to bring in and adapt standards, frameworks, techniques, tools, and processes suitable for one's project. In *Quantum Cybersecurity*, we consider tailoring to adapting within the framework, standard, or method and combining to bring in techniques, tools, and processes from other frameworks, standards, or methods.

Value: technology users' perception of the digital products or services benefits, usefulness and importance that are provided by the organization and is central to ITIL's Service Value System and Service Value Chain.

Vision: the aspiration of what the organization will become in the target (future) state.

Y2K: shortened for the *year 2000* software *problem* where there could have been potential data and system errors when the year turned from 1999 to 2000. Most organizations implemented Y2K projects to safeguard data and systems.

References

Apple Security Research. "iMessage With PQ3: The New State of the Art in Quantum-Secure Messaging at Scale." 2024. https://security.apple.com/blog/imessage-pq3/.

Australian Signals Directorate. "Essential Eight." 2022. Essential Eight | Cyber.gov.au.

Australian Signals Directorate. "Guidance for Managing Risks of Legacy ICT." 2024. www.cyber.gov.au/resources-business-and-government/maintaining-devices-and-systems/system-hardening-and-administration/legacy-ict-management/managing-the-risks-of-legacy-ict-practitioner-guidance#:~:text=Legacy%20information%20communications%20technology%20(ICT,does%20occur%20much%20more%20impactful.

Australian Signals Directorate. "Planning for Post-Quantum Cryptography." 2023. www.cyber.gov.au/resources-business-and-government/governance-and-user-education/governance/planning-post-quantum-cryptography.

AXELOS. *ITIL 4: Digital and IT Strategy*. London: Stationary Office, 2020. ISBN 9780113316489.AXELOS. *ITIL Foundation: ITIL 4 edition*. London: The Stationery Office Ltd, 2019. ISBN 9780113316069.

Baumhof, Andreas. 2019. "The Deal With Quantum Computing and Cryptography." *Infosecurity Magazine*. www.infosecurity-magazine.com/opinions/quantum-computing-cryptography-1-1-1/.

Canadian Centre for Cyber Security. "Preparing Your Organization for the Quantum Threat to Cryptography—ITSAP.00.017." 2021. www.cyber.gc.ca/en/guidance/preparing-your-organization-quantum-threat-cryptography-itsap00017.

Canadian Forum for Digital Infrastructure Resilience (CFDIR) "Canadian National Quantum-Readiness: Best Practices and Guidelines—Version 3." 2023. https://ised-isde.canada.ca/site/spectrum-management-telecommunications/sites/default/files/attachments/2023/cfdir-quantum-readiness-best-practices-v03.pdf.

CEN-CENELEC. "Focus Group on Quantum Technologies." Quantum Technologies Use Cases. 2023. www.cencenelec.eu/media/CEN-CENELEC/AreasOfWork/CEN-CENELEC_Topics/Quantum%20technologies/Documentation%20and%20Materials/fgqt_q05_quantumtechnologiesusecases_release1.pdf.

CISA (Cybersecurity and Infrastructure Security Agency). "National Critical Functions." 2019. www.cisa.gov/sites/default/files/publications/national-critical-functions-overview-508.pdf.

CISA (Cybersecurity and Infrastructure Security Agency). "Quantum-Readiness: Migration to Post-Quantum Cryptography." 2023a. www.cisa.gov/resources-tools/resources/quantum-readiness-migration-post-quantum-cryptography#:~:text=Quantum%2DReadiness%3A%20Migration%20to%20Post%2DQuantum%20Cryptography%20(PQC,technology%20vendors%20to%20discuss%20PQC%2C.

CISA (Cybersecurity and Infrastructure Security Agency). "Cybersecurity Performance Goals." 2023b. www.cisa.gov/cross-sector-cybersecurity-performance-goals.

CISA (Cybersecurity and Infrastructure Security Agency). "Quantum Readiness: Migration to Post-Quantum Cryptography." 2023c. www.cisa.gov/resources-tools/resources/quantum-readiness-migration-post-quantum-cryptography.

Cloud Security Alliance. "Preparing Enterprises for the Quantum Computing Cybersecurity Threats." 2019. https://cloudsecurityalliance.org/artifacts/preparing-enterprises-for-the-quantum-computing-cybersecurity-threats/.

Cloud Security Alliance. "Practical Preparations for the Post-Quantum World." 2021. https://cloudsecurityalliance.org/artifacts/practical-preparations-for-the-post-quantum-world/.

CSIRO. "The Quantum Threat to Cybersecurity: Looking Through the Prism of Post-Quantum Cryptography." 2021. www.math.auckland.ac.nz/~sgal018/CSIRO-PQC-whitepaper.pdf.

Department of Home Affairs. "Enhanced Cyber Security Obligations—Incident Response Planning." 2024. www.cisc.gov.au/resources-subsite/Documents/ecso-guidance-incident-response-planning.pdf.

Einstein, A., B. Max., and B. Hedwig. *The Born-Einstein Letters: Correspondence between Albert Einstein and Max and Hedwig Born from 1916–1955, with Commentaries by Max Born.* London: Macmillan, 1971, p. 158.

Feynman, R.P. "Simulating Physics With Computers." *International Journal of Theoretical Physics,* 21, no. 6 (1982): 467–488. https://doi.org/10.1007/BF02650179.

France, J. "The Race Against Quantum: It's Not Too Late to be the Tortoise That Beat the Har." *InfoSecurity Magazine*, March 7, 2023. www.infosecurity-magazine.com/opinions/race-quantum-tortoise-beat-hare/.

French Cybersecurity Agency. "Should Quantum Key Distribution Be Used for Secure Communications?" 2020. https://cyber.gouv.fr/en/publications/should-quantum-key-distribution-be-used-secure-communications.

FS-ISAC. "Post-Quantum Cryptography (PQC) Working Group: Risk Model Technical Paper." 2023a. www.fsisac.com/hubfs/Knowledge/PQC/RiskModel.pdf.

FS-ISAC. "Post-Quantum Cryptography (PQC) Working Group: Infrastructure Inventory Technical Paper." 2023b. FSISAC-InfrastructureInventory-Final.

GPM. "The GPM® P5™ Standard for Sustainability in Project Management Version 3." 2023. The P5 Standard for Sustainability in Project Management (greenprojectmanagement.org).

Grimes, Roger. "Practical Preparations for the Post-Quantum World, MIT." 2021. https://cams.mit.edu/wp-content/uploads/Grimes-Practical-Preparations -for-the-Post-Quantum-World.pdf.

Hoffbuhr, J.W. "Y2K." *Journal—American Water Works Association* 90, no 9 (1998): 6–6. https://doi.org/10.1002/j.1551-8833.1998.tb08491.x.

IBM. "Security in the Quantum Computing Era." 2023. www.ibm.com/thought -leadership/institute-business-value/en-us/report/quantum-safe-encryption.

Joseph, D., M. Rafael., M. Marc., T. Joe., D.P. Fernando., L. Olivier., L. Stefan., H.Jack.,V. Phil., and H. Royal. 2022. *Transitioning Organizations to Post-Quantum Cryptography. Nature (London)* 605, no. 7909 (2022): 237–243. DOI: 10.1038/s41586-022-04623-2.

KPMG. "Are You Ready for a Quantum Leap?" 2023. https://kpmg.com/us/en/ articles/2023/ready-for-quantum-leap.html.

Mckinsey & Co. "What Is Quantum Computing?" 2023. www.mckinsey.com/ featured-insights/mckinsey-explainers/what-is-quantum-computing#/.

Mosca, M. and M. Piani. "Quantum Threat Timeline Report 2022, Global Risk Institute." 2022. https://globalriskinstitute.org/publication/2022-quantum -threat-timeline-report.

Mosca, M. and M. Piani. 2023. "Quantum Threat Timeline Report 2023, Global Risk Institute." https://globalriskinstitute.org/publication/2023-quantum -threat-timeline-report.

National Cyber Security Centre. "Quantum Security Technologies." 2020. www. ncsc.gov.uk/whitepaper/quantum-security-technologies.

National Security Agency ND. "Quantum Key Distribution (QKD) and Quantum Cryptography (QC)." n.d. www.nsa.gov/Cybersecurity/Quantum -Key-Distribution-QKD-and-Quantum-Cryptography-QC/.

NIST 2003. "Special Publication 800-50: Building an Information Technology Security Awareness and Training Program." Accessed 24 October 2022, https://csrc.nist.gov/publications/detail/sp/800-50/final.

NIST. "Special Publication 800-16, Version 1(3rd Draft): A Role-Based Model for Federal Information Technology/Cybersecurity Training." 2014. https:// csrc.nist.gov/publications/detail/sp/800-16/rev-1/draft.

NIST "Special Publication 800-131 A Revision 2 Transitioning the Use of Cryptographic Algorithms and Key Lengths." 2019. https://csrc.nist.gov/ pubs/sp/800/131/a/r2/final.

NIST. *Special Publication 800-53, Rev. 5: Security and Privacy Controls for Information Systems and Organizations,* September, 2020a. https://doi. org/10.6028/NIST.SP.800-53r5.

NIST. *NIST IR 8286 Integrating Cybersecurity and Enterprise Risk Management (ERM)*, October, 2020b. https://csrc.nist.gov/pubs/ir/8286/final.

NIST. "Getting Ready for Post-Quantum Cryptography: Exploring Challenges Associated With Adopting and Using Post-Quantum Cryptographic Algorithms." 2021. https://csrc.nist.gov/pubs/cswp/15/getting-ready-for-postquantum-cryptography/final.

NIST *"Quantum Readiness: Migration to Post-Quantum Cryptography."* 2023a. www.cisa.gov/sites/default/files/2023-08/Quantum%20Readiness_Final_CLEAR_508c%20%283%29.pdf.

NIST. "NIST Special Publication NIST SP 800-82r3 Guide to Operational Technology (OT) Security." 2023b. https://nvlpubs.nist.gov/nistpubs/SpecialPublications/NIST.SP.800-82r3.pdf.

NIST. "Cybersecurity Capability Maturity Model to NIST Cybersecurity Framework Mapping." 2023c. www.nccoe.nist.gov/news-insights/cybersecurity-capability-maturity-model-nist-cybersecurity-framework-mapping.

NIST. "Public Draft: The NIST Cybersecurity Framework 2.0." August 8, 2023d. https://csrc.nist.gov/News/2023/nist-releases-cybersecurity-framework-2-0-draft.

NIST. "NIST Special Publication 1800-38B Migration to Post-Quantum Cryptography Quantum Readiness: Cryptographic Discovery Volume B: Approach, Architecture, and Security Characteristics of Public Key Application Discovery Tools." 2023e. www.nccoe.nist.gov/sites/default/files/2023-12/pqc-migration-nist-sp-1800-38b-preliminary-draft.pdf.

NIST. "NIST Special Publication 1800-38C Migration to Post-Quantum Cryptography Quantum Readiness: Testing Draft Standards." 2023f. www.nccoe.nist.gov/sites/default/files/2023-12/pqc-migration-nist-sp-1800-38c-preliminary-draft.pdf.

NIST. "Migration to Post-Quantum Cryptography: NIST SP 1800-38A Preliminary Draft Available for Comment." 2023g. www.nccoe.nist.gov/sites/default/files/2023-04/pqc-migration-nist-sp-1800-38a-preliminary-draft.pdf.

NIST. "Cybersecurity Framework (CSF) 2.0." 2024. www.nist.gov/cyberframework.

NSA and CISA. "NSA and CISA Red and Blue Teams Share Top Ten Cybersecurity Misconfigurations." 2023. www.cisa.gov/news-events/cybersecurity-advisories/aa23-278a.

Office of Cybersecurity, Energy Security, and Emergency Response. *Cybersecurity Capability Maturity Model (C2M2)*, US Department of Energy, 2022. Accessed January 22, 2023. www.energy.gov/ceser/cybersecurity-capability-maturity-model-c2m2.

Perryman, A., A. Bocharnikov., C. Lim., and K. Chakraborty.2024. "Improving Tomorrow's Security by Decoding the Quantum Computing Threat." www.ey.com/en_au/cybersecurity/improving-tomorrow-s-security-by-decoding-the-quantum-computing-threat.

Project Management Institute. *Agile Practice Guide*. Newtown Square, PA: Project Management Institute. 2017.

Project Management Institute. *Organizational Project Management Maturity Model (OPM3): Knowledge Foundation*. Newtown Square, PA: Project Management Institute, 2003.

Project Management Institute *The Standard for Program Management—Fourth Edition*. 4th edition. Newtown Square, PA: Project Management Institute. 2017.

Pupillo, L., A. Ferreira., V. Lipiainien., and C. Polito. *Quantum Technologies and Cybersecurity: Technology, Governance and Policy Challenges*. Task Force Report. Brussels: Centre for European Policy Studies. www.ceps.eu/ceps-publications/quantum-technologies-and-cybersecurity/.

Schwaber, K. and S. Jeff. "The Scrum Guide™." *Scrum Guides*. 2017. Accessed November 20, 2022. https://scrumguides.org/.

Shor, P. W. "Algorithms for Quantum Computation: Discrete Logarithms and Factoring." In *Proceedings 35th Annual Symposium on Foundations of Computer Science*, Santa Fe, NM, USA, 124–134, DOI: 10.1109/SFCS.1994.365700.

Skulmoski, G. and C. Walker. *Cybersecurity Training: A Pathway to Readiness*. NY, New York: Business Expert Press, 2023. ISBN-13: 978-1-63742-553-4.

Skulmoski, G. and A. Memari. "Get Ready for the Next Generation of AI Quantum Technologies." In *Voices of Innovation-AI*, ed E. Marx (HIMSS Book Series. Taylor & Francis Group, In Press, 2024).Skulmoski, G. *Shields Up: Cybersecurity Project Management*. NY, New York: Business Expert Press, 2022. ISBN: 978-1-63742-290-8.

Tett, G. "Encryptogeddon Is Coming For Us All." *FT Magazine*. June 1, 2022, www.ft.com/content/a8204a7d-2922-4944-bdff-5449a8f3aee9.

The White House "National Security Memorandum on Promoting United States Leadership in Quantum Computing While Mitigating Risks to Vulnerable Cryptographic Systems." May 4, 2022. www.whitehouse.gov/briefing-room/statements-releases/2022/05/04/national-security-memorandum-on-promoting-united-states-leadership-in-quantum-computing-while-mitigating-risks-to-vulnerable-cryptographic-systems/.

TNO (Nederlandse Organisatie voor toegepast-natuurwetenschappelijk onderzoek). "The PQC Migration Handbook: Guidelines for Migrating to Post-Quantum Cryptography, Applied Cryptography and Quantum Algorithms and CWI – Cryptology Group and AIVD-Netherlands National Communications Security Agency." 2023. www.marc-stevens.nl/research/papers/2023_PQC_Migration_Handbook.pdf.

Tsunoda, H. and K. Yasunobau. "Evaluation of Detailed CSFs and Benefits Model for ITIL Implementation." *International Journal of Innovation, Management and Technology* 9, no 4 (2018): 145–151. doi:10.18178/ijimt.2018.9.4.804.

Verenacchia, S. "Quantum Leap: Advancing a Strategy for Quantum Computing That Will Inspire, Support and Safeguard Economic Growth in the Middle East." PWC. World Government Summit 2019. www.pwc.com/m1/en/world-government-summit/documents/wgs-quantum-leap.pdf.

World Economic Forum. "State of Quantum Computing: Building a Quantum Economy." 2022a. WEF_State_of_Quantum_Computing_2022.pdf (weforum.org).

World Economic Forum. "Transitioning to a Quantum-Secure Economy." 2022b. www3.weforum.org/docs/WEF_Transitioning%20to_a_Quantum_Secure_Economy_2022.pdf.

About the Authors

Greg Skulmoski, **PhD, MBA, BEd, CITP, FBCS,** is an award-winning project manager who teaches project and risk management at Bond University, Australia. Greg brings 15 years of complex and emerging technologies project experience in the Middle East and Canada.

Ashkan Memari, PhD, MEng, BEng, FHEA, is an academic and researcher at Central Queensland University in Australia, with international experience spanning the Middle East, South Asia, and Australia. Ashkan's primary research area revolves around sustainability and is in the top 10 most cited works globally.

Index

OTHER TITLES IN THE PORTFOLIO AND PROJECT MANAGEMENT COLLECTION

Timothy J. Kloppenborg, Xavier University and
Kam Jugdev, Athabasca University, Editors

- *Creating Value Through Project-Based Supply Chain Decisions* by Denise Chenger
- *Project Teams, Second Edition* by Vittal S. Anantatmula
- *Lead Then Learn* by Annie MacLeod
- *Tune-Up Your Small Business* by Raewyn Sleeman
- *The Professional Project Manager* by Carsten Laugesen
- *The Agile Enterprise* by David Asch
- *A Project Sponsor's Warp-Speed Guide* by Yogi Schulz and Jocelyn Lapointe
- *Power Skills That Lead to Exceptional Performance* by Neal Whitten
- *Great Meetings Build Great Teams* by Rich Maltzman and Jim Stewart
- *When Graduation's Over, Learning Begins* by Roger Forsgren
- *Project Control Methods and Best Practices* by Yakubu Olawale
- *Managing Projects With PMBOK 7* by James Marion and Tracey Richardson
- *Shields Up* by Gregory J. Skulmoski
- *Greatness in Construction History* by Sherif Hashem
- *The Inner Building Blocks* by Abhishek Rai

Concise and Applied Business Books

The Collection listed above is one of 30 business subject collections that Business Expert Press has grown to make BEP a premiere publisher of print and digital books. Our concise and applied books are for...

- Professionals and Practitioners
- Faculty who adopt our books for courses
- Librarians who know that BEP's Digital Libraries are a unique way to offer students ebooks to download, not restricted with any digital rights management
- Executive Training Course Leaders
- Business Seminar Organizers

Business Expert Press books are for anyone who needs to dig deeper on business ideas, goals, and solutions to everyday problems. Whether one print book, one ebook, or buying a digital library of 110 ebooks, we remain the affordable and smart way to be business smart. For more information, please visit www.businessexpertpress.com, or contact sales@businessexpertpress.com.

www.ingramcontent.com/pod-product-compliance
Lightning Source LLC
Chambersburg PA
CBHW061215220326
41599CB00025B/4649